Getting the Measure of Money

GETTING THE MEASURE OF MONEY

A Critical Assessment of
UK Monetary Indicators

ANTHONY J. EVANS

Institute of
Economic Affairs

First published in Great Britain in 2018 by
The Institute of Economic Affairs
2 Lord North Street
Westminster
London SW1P 3LB
in association with London Publishing Partnership Ltd
www.londonpublishingpartnership.co.uk

The mission of the Institute of Economic Affairs is to improve understanding of the fundamental institutions of a free society by analysing and expounding the role of markets in solving economic and social problems.

A CIP catalogue record for this book is available from the British Library.

ISBN 978-0-255-36767-7

Many IEA publications are translated into languages other than English or are reprinted. Permission to translate or to reprint should be sought from the Director General at the address above.

Typeset in Kepler by T&T Productions Ltd
www.tandtproductions.com

Printed and bound in Great Britain by Hobbs the Printers Ltd

CONTENTS

THE AUTHOR

Anthony J. Evans is Professor of Economics at ESCP Europe Business School. He has published in a range of academic and trade journals and is the author of *Markets for Managers* (Wiley, 2014). His work has been covered by most broadsheet newspapers, and he has appeared on *Newsnight* and the BBC World Service. He is part of the MOC Affiliate Faculty for the Institute for Strategy and Competitiveness at Harvard Business School, and is a member of the Institute of Economic Affairs' Shadow Monetary Policy Committee. He is a UEFA qualified soccer coach and lives in Hertfordshire with his wife and two children.

PREFACE

My efforts to learn about the link between monetary economics and macroeconomic fluctuations received three important boosts. The first occurred during my PhD at George Mason University. There, I was granted an incredible opportunity to learn about Austrian economics from some of its most knowledgeable advocates. I took classes from the likes of Peter J. Boettke and Richard E. Wagner, and attended a graduate reading group led by Christopher J. Coyne and Scott Beaulier. This helped me to transition from being an enthusiastic (albeit quiet) consumer of ideas to an eclectic (but published) producer. It focused my attention on how to become a professional academic and laid a broad foundation of interests and expertise. Then, while I was writing up my dissertation I met Toby Baxendale, an entrepreneur based in the UK. This was fortuitous for two reasons. Firstly, it led to an appointment at ESCP Europe Business School, providing me with a rewarding job in an incredible institution. Secondly, it coincided with a peaking housing boom and the early stages of the 2008 financial crisis. At the time, I felt that I had a basic theoretical toolkit that helped me to understand what was going on – it seemed obvious that this was an Austrian-style trade cycle, and that the Austrian school was on the cusp of a major resurgence. But Toby gave me a perspective and attitude that helped me to seize on this. His ceaseless drive encouraged me to see myself as a champion of Austrian ideas, and not drift into academic irrelevance. And his generous cooperation not only educated me on points of theory, but also helped me view the Austrian approach in a new way – its importance stems not from its internal coherence, but because it allows us to navigate the real world. The events of the summer of 2008 drew my attention and I felt a professional obligation to become a spokesperson for the Austrian school in the UK. It led to several newspaper articles, policy work and public talks.

However, my aim has always been to be 'a good economist' rather than 'a good Austrian economist', and I was conscious of gaps in my understanding. The third boost to my efforts came in 2011 when I was Fulbright-Scholar-in-Residence at San Jose State University and had the chance to audit a graduate class on monetary theory given by Jeffrey Rogers Hummel. This, more than anything else, set my standards on the depth of knowledge necessary to call oneself a monetary economist. I found it a liberating experience – personally and professionally – to encounter some of the classic works in monetary theory. While I was there, I was also privileged to join the Institute of Economic Affairs' Shadow Monetary Policy Committee (SMPC). This requires a monthly contribution to a high-quality policy discussion with some of the best and most revered economists in the country. Throughout my career I have made attempts to associate myself with knowledgeable people from whom I can learn. I have regularly presented at conferences such as the Southern Economic Association,

Eastern Economic Association and Association of Private Enterprise Education, and set up Kaleidic Economics to serve as a regular business roundtable and basis for the publication of my non-academic reports and data. But those three main experiences (at GMU, in London and in California) over the course of a decade, made me feel that I could make a contribution to Austrian monetary economics. This book is the result.

ACKNOWLEDGEMENTS

I gratefully acknowledge helpful advice and feedback from Toby Baxendale, Peter Boettke, Philip Booth, Sam Bowman, Kevin Dowd, Jeffrey Rogers Hummel, Robert Miller, Nick Schandler, George Selgin, Mark Skousen, Ben Southwood, Robert Thorpe, Lawrence H. White and Jamie Whyte. Their collective wisdom is compelling and radical, and I have done my best to draw upon it.

I'm aware of the danger that the book may be too complicated for the non-economist, too academic for the practitioner and too simplistic for monetary theorists. All I can say is that I believe attention towards all three audiences is a noble goal, regardless of whether I reach it. According to G. L. S. Shackle, 'Hayek opened a window and showed us a beautiful vista. Then he shut it' (see Littlechild 2000: 340). I can't claim to have reopened that window. But I have caught glimpses of the view, and hope this book aids others to see even more.

SUMMARY

- The Monetary Policy Committee of the Bank of England's reliance on faulty indicators has led to suboptimal policy decisions and masked what is actually happening in the economy.
- The introduction of quantitative easing (QE) in 2009 has made the money supply relevant again and made a discussion about alternative money supply measures of direct policy significance. Unfortunately, official Bank of England figures have proved misleading and subject to major alterations (such as the replacement of M4 with M4ex).
- This book argues in favour of measures such as MZM and Divisia money, which attempt to find a middle ground between narrow and broad measures. It introduces a new and publicly available measure, MA, based on an a priori approach to defining money as the generally accepted medium of exchange.
- Central bankers are right to alter monetary policy in light of changes in the demand for money (i.e. velocity shocks), but they also need to recognise the potential for their own actions to be the cause of such shocks.
- In particular, central banks are 'big players' who can weaken confidence by generating regime uncertainty, and this played a major role in the 2008 financial crisis.

- While increased attention to uncertainty by economists should be welcomed, we should also be wary of attempts to measure it.
- From 1999 to 2006 the Consumer Prices Index (CPI) systematically underreported the inflationary pressure in the UK. More attention should be given to indices that include asset prices.
- GDP figures available at the time understated the severity of the 2008 recession, but also understated the strength of the recovery.
- GDP is flawed as a measure of well-being, of economic growth and even of economic activity. We get a fuller picture if we include intermediate consumption (or business-to-business spending), which is known as 'Gross Output' (GO).
- GO for the UK is typically two times bigger than GDP and more volatile. Unfortunately, official figures are only published on an annual basis and with a significant lag.

TABLES AND FIGURES[1]

---

1   All author data is available at http://econ.anthonyjevans.com/books/
    mvpy/

1 INTRODUCTION

From a practical point of view, it would be one of the
worst things that would befall us if the general public
should ever cease to believe in the elementary proposi-
tions of the quantity theory.

Hayek (1931: 199)

When the Bank of England was made independent in 1997,
conventional monetary policy was straightforward. Often
referred to as 'One Target One Tool', the mandate given
to the Monetary Policy Committee (MPC) was clear: use
interest rates (the tool) to hit 2.0 per cent inflation (the
target). When the global financial crisis struck, however,
conventional monetary policy seemed to fail. Interest
rates were cut to the zero lower bound, and alternative
policy objectives (such as lower unemployment) became
more pertinent. Therefore the MPC launched an array of
additional tools (such as quantitative easing and forward
guidance), while only paying lip service to inflation. A new
era of emergency monetary policy began and even a decade
later shows no signs of retreating. From a distance there's
an appearance of flying by the seat of one's pants, and a
lack of confidence in the underlying monetary framework.

The flaws of conventional monetary policy have been exposed. But, as yet, we haven't settled on an alternative.

This book contends that the MPC has not lost as much control as it may appear. Rather, an over-reliance on faulty indicators has led to suboptimal policy decisions and masked what is actually happening in the economy. As contemporary macroeconomics becomes ever more complex, and as monetary policy becomes ever more ad hoc, we need an anchor: something simple and robust to orient ourselves around. And the 'equation of exchange' can provide this.

The equation of exchange is a simple model showing the relationship between various economic aggregates, and has been understood and utilised by classical economists such as Richard Cantillon, David Hume and John Stuart Mill. It was most famously adopted in algebraic form by Irving Fisher, in 1911, as follows:

$$MV = PT.$$

Here, M refers to the stock of money, V the velocity of circulation, P the general price level, and T the total number of transactions. The power of the model can be seen by the amount of debate it has generated, with various scholars and schools of thought adopting their own favoured versions. For example, the Cambridge approach of Arthur Cecil Pigou, Dennis Robertson and John Maynard Keynes challenged the concept of 'velocity' (emphasising instead the demand for money) and claimed that income (Y) was more relevant than transactions. Accompanying the rise of Keynesian macroeconomics we also saw the blossoming of national income accounts, where (according to the circular flow model) income (Y) and final output (Q) are the same. The newfound ability to measure these terms turned the equation of exchange from an abstract theoretical apparatus into a useful policy tool. By the time Milton Friedman pioneered the version typically used today ($MV = PY$), it was driven by empirical considerations as opposed to theoretical purity. This focuses attention on whether the Consumer Prices Index (CPI) is the optimal measure of inflation, or if GDP fully captures the structure of the economy. It is time for an update.

The aim of this book is to disassemble the equation of exchange and critique conventional monetary indicators. It uses a dynamic version of the equation, where the variables are growth rates rather than levels.[1] In other words:

$$M + V = P + Y.$$

M refers to the growth rate of the money supply, while V is the velocity of circulation. P is inflation and Y is real output growth.

How the money supply is measured, the components of the demand for money, the means of calculating price indices, and the pros and cons of GDP: each has its own fascinating history.[2] The ambition of this book is more modest. It is merely to critique the way the four terms are usually measured.

---

1   For more on the origins of the dynamic version, see Evans (2016b).

2   Coyle (2014) is a fine example of an intellectual history of one of these variables.

Chapter 2 takes a subjectivist, a priori approach to provide a coherent definition of money and then charts recent changes in the UK. This measure of the money supply is termed 'MA' and is a middle ground between narrow and broad monetary aggregates. The chapter critically assesses similar attempts to measure the money supply (such as TMS and AMS), as well as close substitutes such as Divisia money.

Chapter 3 argues that central bank actions (especially during financial crises) can generate regime uncertainty and that this constitutes a velocity shock. The concept of 'supplier-induced demand' is used to argue that monetary contractions are not the only way that central bank incompetence can cause recessions. Attempts to measure uncertainty are assessed along with the monetary channels through which uncertainty operates. The chapter also argues that instead of viewing velocity as a mere residual in the equation of exchange, its inverse – the demand for money – allows us to put individual choice and subjectivism at the core of our monetary theory.

Chapter 4 attempts to uncover the potential for credit booms to occur during a period of stable consumer prices. It provides a critique of the Consumer Prices Index (CPI) as a measure of inflation, a discussion of growth versus level targets, and surveys the failure of the Bank of England's own inflation fan charts. A productivity norm is calculated to reveal some of the hidden inflation that occurred in the build-up to the crisis, revealing that the 'Great Moderation' was partly a myth.

Chapter 5 looks at GDP in terms of capital theory, and contrasts it with alternatives such as net national product

(NNP) and net private product remaining (NPPR). It also provides a detailed look at the theoretical basis for including intermediate consumption, and gives more attention to the productive side of the economy when looking at measures of economic activity. This leads to an estimate of 'gross output' using input–output data, and incorporates data from the UK Payments Council to estimate total transactions.

The conclusion draws this all together. It looks at inflationary booms and explains the upper limit to widespread resource misallocation. But it also looks at deflationary spirals (including the theory of 'debt-deflation' and 'cumulative rot') and provides an understanding of the lower limit to economic depressions.

Using the equation of exchange as a framework we can make some contributions to the policy debate about the causes of macroeconomic fluctuations. Monetarists will emphasise contractions in monetary aggregates (i.e. M), while Keynesians will focus more on the volatility of animal spirits (i.e. V). Both identify the instability of aggregate demand $(M + V)$ as the problem. By contrast, real business cycle theorists will point to the supply side of the economy and highlight changes in real productivity growth (i.e. Y).[3] Each of these approaches contains important insights and is relevant depending on the circumstances of time and place. In the chapters that follow there are two crucial policy implications that emerge. One is that supply-side

---

3 I credit Jeffrey Rogers Hummel for linking the equation of exchange to alternative business cycle theories in this way.

shocks (i.e. changes in Y) should be revealed in P. The other is that in order to reduce the load on the price system, changes in V should be offset by changes in M.

Quantity theory is an attempt to explain movements in prices through changes in the quantity of money, and neatly demonstrates the usefulness of the equation of exchange as a basis for making causal arguments. If V and Y are reasonably stable over time, then any increase in M must manifest itself in higher P. Quantity theory has generated debates about whether or not causality runs from the left side of the equation to the right, whether V is independent of M, or whether Y is driven by real factors (as opposed to monetary ones). These debates demonstrate the strength of the equation of exchange as an underlying basis for understanding the economy.[4]

Although the methodological approach taken in this book is somewhat heterodox, it fits into the rich history of casual empiricism. My aim is to use evidence to illustrate and illuminate an *identity*, rather than subject a specified *theory* to econometric testing. I am not going beyond empirical relationships based on correlation and intuition, or a criterion based on what Leland Yeager (1997: 249) referred to as 'explanatory power and conformity to fact and logic'. This isn't to say that robust statistical tests are not important, but that they require theoretically sound data series as an *input*. This book is a step towards improving

---

4   In the rest of the book I will use quantity theory and the equation of exchange interchangeably, as is the common habit. It should be clear, though, that doing so does not imply a monetarist perspective or make any causal assumptions.

the inputs. I am not claiming to have created new indicators that are better than traditional ones. But as a dissident casual empiricist, my aim is to challenge prevalent indicators, understand their flaws, and then present the implications for monetary policy. Debates about the potential slowdown in productivity growth are fundamentally informed by our understanding of aggregate variables. We cannot expect improvements in decision-making unless the indicators reflect what is actually going on.

2 M: THE IMPORTANCE OF ALTERNATIVE MONETARY AGGREGATES

Summary of key points

- For some time academic economists have neglected the role of money, and monetary policy has been conducted through interest rates rather than the money supply.
- The introduction of quantitative easing (QE) in 2009 has made the money supply relevant again, and made a discussion about alternative money supply measures of direct policy significance. Unfortunately, official Bank of England figures have proved misleading and subject to major alterations (such as the replacement of M4 with M4ex).
- This chapter argues in favour of measures such as MZM and Divisia money, which attempt to find a middle ground between narrow and broad, and introduces a new and publicly available measure, MA, based on an a priori approach to defining money as the generally accepted medium of exchange.
- Attention to MA would have provided an early warning that a major credit crunch was occurring in 2008, and explains the lethargic recovery.

Introduction

The conventional explanation for the cause of the Great Depression was an unprecedented contraction of the money supply (Friedman and Schwartz 1963b; Romer 1992). So when, in 2008, many of us were concerned that the recent housing boom would precede an imminent credit crunch, monetary aggregates seemed an obvious place to look for warning signs. And yet M4 (the conventional measure of broad money for the UK) was growing strongly. The growth rate increased from around 9 per cent in 2004 to 14 per cent by 2007. And then, in late 2008, it went above 17 per cent. At the time, I was working on compiling an alternative measure of the money supply, and my measure showed a dramatic contraction. Something seemed amiss.

In September 2007 the Bank of England had begun a user consultation to modify M4, proposing to exclude intermediate 'other financial corporations' (OFCs) because it views them as containing interbank transfers.[1] This was timely because QE boosted the money holdings of intermediate OFCs, but it was only in May 2009 that the Bank released quarterly estimates of M4 that excluded those intermediate OFCs (see Janssen 2009). In stark contrast to the existing M4, M4ex now showed a dramatic fall in broad money from mid 2008 (see Figure 1).[2] As David B. Smith

---

1   See Burgess and Janssen (2007). As Ward (2011) says, 'the exclusion is justified because the money holdings of such institutions are unrelated to economic transactions'.

2   I appreciate help from Norbert Janssen to create Figure 1. Series codes: LPQVQJW quarterly 12-month growth rate of M4 (monetary financial

(2010: 2) said, 'unfortunately for the Bank of England, the renewed emphasis on broad money occurred when its established M4 definition had become distorted by artificial transactions designed to push bank liabilities off balance sheet'.

Figure 1   M4 and M4ex, 1998–2009 (year-on-year % change)

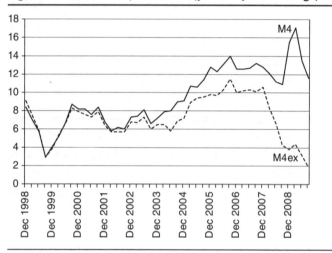

This timing had a major impact on policy decisions. At the height of the financial crisis, in September 2008, there was an almost divergent relationship between the traditional measure of broad money (M4) and a new measure

institutions' sterling M4 liabilities to private sector) (in per cent) seasonally adjusted; and RPQB56Q quarterly 12-month growth rate of UK resident monetary financial institutions' (excluding the central bank) sterling M4 liabilities to private sector excluding intermediate OFCs (in per cent) seasonally adjusted.

of broad money (M4ex) that the Bank was attempting to launch. Even the Governor of the Bank of England seemed confused. In 2011 Mervyn King advocated QE2 on the grounds that the money supply was falling. But while this was true for M4 (which fell by 0.6 per cent relative to the previous year), M4ex had increased by 2.2 per cent (Ward 2011). He was looking at the wrong measure of broad money.

Other events compounded the lack of data. In September 2008 the Bank was concerned that confidentiality issues would emerge following the inclusion of the recently nationalised Northern Rock in the ONS Public Sector Finance Statistics (PSF). To prevent market watchers from arbitraging information between different data sources, a specific table (A3.2) was discontinued. It was reinstated in June 2009, because by then other banks had been brought into the public sector. But for several critical months we lost information. Similarly, in the US, William Barnett (2012: 27) has pointed out that the Federal Reserve not only stopped reporting M3 in March 2006, but also stopped releasing the component series. When the Bank of England began paying interest on reserves in May 2006, it switched from M0 to 'Notes and Coin' as its favoured measure of the narrow money supply. There may well be valid reasons for such changes, but the timing was unfortunate. It was like a boat heading into stormy waters while experimenting with new navigational equipment.

The global financial crisis has had a profound and enduring impact on the way monetary policy has been conducted. In March 2009, the Bank of England reduced the Bank rate to 0.5 per cent, which has been seen as a lower bound for policy, limiting the scope for further cuts. In conjunction with this decision it was announced that £75 billion worth of quantitative easing (QE) would be launched, intending to inject money directly into the economy through the purchase of various financial assets with newly created reserves.[3] In addition to demonstrating a change in focus from short-term to longer-term interest rates, QE has also increased the attention paid to the role of monetary aggregates. As the then Governor, Mervyn King, explicitly revealed, 'We are now doing [this] in order to increase the supply of broad money in the economy'.[4] Despite theoretical and empirical doubts about the ability to define and measure the money supply, it is of direct and increasing policy significance.

This is in stark contrast to previous trends that have downplayed attention to the money supply. The US Federal Reserve stopped targeting M1 in 1987 and M2 in 1992. Financial deregulation that occurred during this period was seen to create greater instability in the demand for money, and thus reduce the influence of the money supply on prices and output. Indeed 'the reliability of various money measures as useful indicators on which to base policy has become seriously compromised' (Carlson and Keen 1996: 15). As already mentioned, in March 2006 the Fed ceased to even publish figures for M3 and in May 2006 the Bank of

---

3   In November 2009 this was increased to £200 billion and in May 2014 stood at £375 billion.

4   Comments made to the Treasury Select Committee, quoted by Cohen (2009).

England replaced M0 (with 'Notes and Coin'). These decisions suggest that either the money supply does not matter, or that even if it does we cannot reliably measure it. This chapter maintains that the money supply *does* matter, but that existing measures fail. The debate between 'narrow' and 'broad' measures, and work on Divisia approaches, lack a coherent definition of money.

This chapter tries to do two things, firstly provide a coherent definition of money and secondly identify recent changes in the UK money supply. This discussion will be used as a basis for analysing traditional measures of the money supply and other measures from the a priori tradition. The measure being proposed, labelled 'MA', finds evidence to support the conventional wisdom that a sustained and increasing monetary expansion during the Great Moderation was followed in 2008 by a catastrophic slowdown in money creation that became a sustained monetary contraction. The first section asks whether money can be measured, drawing attention to notions of emergence and subjectivity. The second section surveys existing Austrian school attempts to measure the money supply, and presents a measure called MA. The third section shows how MA differs from conventional measures of the UK money supply. The final section discusses Divisia monetary aggregates and how they relate to MA.

Can money be measured?

Two aspects of money make it difficult to measure: its *emergent* properties and its inherent *subjectivism*. The characterisation of money as an emergent, social institution originates from Menger (1892). A barter system has high transaction costs and therefore certain commodities that were universally valued emerged to satisfy the so-called double coincidence of wants. Money emerged as a social institution to facilitate economic exchange (see Mises 1912: 45). I will define money through this unique role. That is, I define money as a *generally accepted medium of exchange* – money is what all goods and services are traded in exchange for.[5] As the final payment for all goods, money is one half of all economic exchanges and thus cannot have a market of its own. This explains why monetary disequilibrium has such far-reaching consequences: any adjustments in the exchange value of money must be felt across all markets (Yeager 1997; Horwitz 2000: 67). Thus (Yeager 1997: 88):

---

5   This follows the definition typically used by Austrian economists (Rothbard 1978: 144; Salerno 1987: 1; White 1992: 204). This definition is not free from ambiguity, however. The emergence of contactless payment technology (which allows account holders to hover their debit card over a reader, rather than have to enter the card into the machine and then enter a PIN number) demonstrates that cash and debit cards are not perfect substitutes. Slightly reducing the transaction costs of using debit cards creates value and makes them more like cash. But it is not necessarily the case that cash will always be a closer fit to this definition than deposit accounts. Historically, some mail order companies only accepted cheques (and not cash). The rise of internet shopping has led to the emergence of companies such as PayPal that profit from the fact that electronic payments are more secure and easier to compute than using hard cash. For online payments, current accounts are more marketable than cash. One might think that legal tender laws mitigate this point, by mandating what people are legally obliged to accept, but they only apply within certain ranges. Robert Fitzpatrick found this to his cost when he attempted to pay a debt of £804 using 1p and 2p coins. These low denomination coppers are only legal tender for goods costing a maximum of 20p (Cocozza 2012).

An excess demand for actual money shows itself to individual economic units less clearly than does an excess of demand for any other thing, including the nearest of near moneys. It eliminates itself more indirectly and with more momentous macroeconomic consequences.

To say that money is a medium of exchange does not deny that it performs other functions, such as a store of value, unit of account, standard of deferred payment and means of final payment. But these should be considered as secondary (or derived) functions. Nor does defining money as a medium of exchange mean that people demand it only for transaction purposes. The utility provided by money is multi-faceted and impossible to neatly separate into different 'motives'.

It might appear as though the emergent properties of money impede one's ability to neatly categorise it, since emergent phenomena change over time. And as Horwitz (1990: 462) says, 'financial assets have degrees of "moneyness" about them, and ... different financial assets can be placed along a moneyness continuum'. However, it is precisely these emergent properties that tend to deliver a focal point of relatively few commonly accepted media of exchange. The fact that the value of money derives from its use in exchange implies that people will tend to coordinate around the same currencies.[6] Network effects and

---

6   As Friedman and Schwartz (1970: 136) point out, 'there is some ambiguity in the specific assets that serve as literal media of exchange; and the assets that serve this function will differ from time to time and place to place ... but for any one time and place the ambiguity is likely to be confined to a narrow range'.

switching costs can be expected to deliver some stability over time.[7]

Measurement is also hampered by the inherent subjectivity of what constitutes money. Since the value of money is a function of an expectation about what other people will accept as a means of payment, there is no a priori means to identify 'money'.[8] Whatever emerges as the general medium is based more on historical or cultural factors than any 'intrinsic' suitability. While gold possesses several characteristics that make it appropriate (such as durability and fungibility), there is nothing to say that in different contexts other commodities would not be used (e.g. cigarettes, see Radford 1945). Consequently, any attempt to measure the money supply is essentially a historical survey. Researchers must ascertain which commodities were being used as the 'generally accepted' medium of exchange and cannot rely on objective definitions. You can only truly measure money retrospectively, as we know whether people's expectation of what would be accepted in exchange were accurate.

Despite these difficulties, the classification and measurement of the money supply is possible. And two further

---

7   I thank an anonymous referee for adding this point.

8   Note that 'generally accepted' is a looser criterion than 'universally accepted'. It just means that it is routinely accepted, and that there is a reasonable expectation that it will be accepted. Money is not just a subjective phenomenon but is also an intersubjective one. As Yeager (1997: 100) points out, accepting something in exchange does not make it a medium of exchange – the recipient may have become an agent who converts it into money at a later date. Hence the importance of a medium of exchange that is *generally accepted*.

reasons suggest this is feasible. Firstly, the existing monetary regime does not really permit money to emerge spontaneously, and thus what constitutes money is relatively stable. This is because of the legal tender laws and other state interventions that impose a definition of money on the market. With a monopoly issuer of base currency and a central banking system, the task of measuring the money supply is largely reduced to the task of defining money. Provided the definition of money is well grounded, it is mostly a case of sorting through official statistics. The challenges involved in identifying exactly *which* assets are being used as the medium of exchange is made significantly easier due to state intervention. Secondly, the feasibility of measuring the money supply is a judgment based on the next best alternative. Given that academics, policymakers and commentators all use existing measures, there is an element of pragmatism at play. Current measures should serve as the benchmark to judge new measures, as opposed to a theoretically 'pure' abstraction. We cannot perfectly measure national income either, but that doesn't mean that all attempts are equally bad.

This a priori method intends to provide a clear and conceptually solid definition of 'money' and then search for measures of any and all asset classes that fall into this classification.[9] In a response to Milton Friedman's attempts to measure monetary aggregates, White (1992: 204) says, 'there may be some practical difficulty in

---

9   This is not to say that 'the' money supply is the only monetary aggregate that is of interest. For example it would be useful to monitor how 'near moneys' ebb and flow as the money supply changes.

identifying or counting the units of money … in an economy. But this does not bear on the proper choice of a definition of money'. Indeed, 'the purpose of a definition of money is not to make the statisticians measurements as easy as possible, but to help them be as meaningful as possible' (ibid.: 208). Friedman and Schwartz (1970) seem to claim that since money is hard to measure, it is hard to define. But this need not follow. What constitutes money is likely to change over time, but the definition of money should not. We can use an a priori *definition*, but a historically convenient *measure*.

There are two main alternatives to an a priori approach, both of which are inductive. One is to focus on the substitutability between asset classes, while the other simply seeks whatever fits the historic data the best (see Yeager 1970: 88). This reflects a wider methodological divide within the economics profession, and Friedman and Schwartz (1970) contrast the a priori approach of people such as Tooke and Cannan with an empirical approach followed by Keynes, Marshall and Robertson. While an a priori approach will judge MA based on its conceptual coherence, a more inductive approach will judge it on its predictive ability. The focus is on the theoretical validity of the measure, and the data are provided as a *cautious* justification of its relevance.

Austrian definitions of the money supply

Given that Austrian school economists tend to emphasise tight analytical (or a priori) reasoning and the primacy of theoretical soundness over empirical testing, it is no surprise that economists working within this tradition tend to place greater emphasis on 'an explicit and coherent theoretical conception of the essential nature of money' (Salerno 1987: 1), as opposed to 'an arbitrary mixing of various liquid assets' (Shostak 2000: 69).

The seminal attempt to create a distinct Austrian measure of the money supply was advocated by Murray Rothbard (1978: 153), and is defined as the following:

> Total supply of cash held in the banks + total demand deposits + total savings deposits in commercial and savings banks + total shares in savings and loan associations + time deposits and small CDs at current redemption rates + total policy reserves of life insurance companies – policy loans outstanding – demand deposits owned by savings banks, saving and loan associations, and life insurance companies + savings bonds, at current rates of redemption.

Drawing heavily upon this, Joseph Salerno devised the 'True Money Supply' (Salerno 1987), the components of which are:

> Currency Component of M1, Total Checkable Deposits, Savings Deposits, U.S. Government Demand Deposits and Note Balances, Demand Deposits Due to Foreign Commercial Banks, and Demand Deposits Due to Foreign Official Institutions.

The TMS used to be publicly available via the Mises Institute.[10] Figure 2 shows the year-on-year percentage change in TMS from 2004 to 2011.

Figure 2   True Money Supply

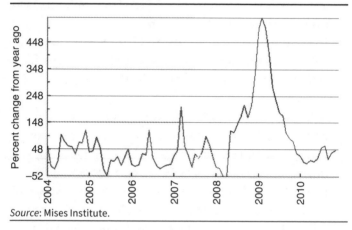

Source: Mises Institute.

The first point to make is that it is very volatile. Before the financial crisis it grew by 92 per cent in August 2005 and fell by 52 per cent in November. In July 2009 it peaked at a growth rate of 538 per cent and yet in August 2010 it was contracting. Secondly, despite going back to 1959 the series was last updated in April 2011. Also, I have attempted to replicate the TMS and was unable to do so.[11]

---

10 http://mises.org/content/nofed/chart.aspx?series=TMS (accessed 25 May 2014).

11 To replicate the TMS I used the following FRED series (monthly, not seasonally adjusted): CURRNS, TCDNS, SAVINGNS, DDDFCBNS, DDDFOINS, USGVDDNS. This perfectly replicates TMS from 1998–2000, after which a

White (1992) provides an alternative way to measure the money supply, which essentially amounts to M1 plus money market deposit accounts (MMDAs), containing the following elements:

Currency; Travellers checks; Checkable claims on banks

White's discussion is theoretically rigorous but he doesn't attempt to provide a measure. The 'Austrian Money Supply' (AMS) is outlined by Shostak (2000) and was published by Man Financial. The three main components of the AMS are:

Cash; demand deposits with commercial banks and thrift institutions; government deposits with banks and the central bank.

Finally, Diapason Commodities and Morgan Stanley have also published close versions of the AMS as part of sub-scription-based investment reports.

The main difference between the TMS and AMS is that the TMS includes certain types of savings accounts, and since savings constitute over 70 per cent of the TMS this has a large effect.[12] An advantage of AMS is that it has a UK version, but the series used are not public information. I

difference of $1 billion exists, rising to $20 billion in 2005, $30 billion in late 2007/early 2008, but then the error term disappears by the end of 2008. I have been unable to understand the reason for these discrepancies.

12 See Hummel (2014) for more differences between Rothbard, Salerno and Shostak's methods.

have had difficulty replicating it.[13] Pollaro (2010) provided a lengthy discussion of money-supply metrics from an Austrian perspective and created two measures: TMS1 (based on Shostak) and TMS2 (based on Rothbard and Salerno). These were regularly published on Forbes.com but stopped in 2014.[14]

It is telling that the details of either the TMS or AMS have not been published in a peer-reviewed journal, and there are several reasons why this may be the case. Partly, this is because recent interest in money supply measures tends to be driven by professional rather than academic economists (although the final section of this chapter will show that Divisia measures seem to be changing this). Less importance is therefore attached to a peer-review process. Methods may also be more guarded for commercial reasons. But the bottom line is that not only are there conceptual issues with how TMS and AMS are defined: interested observers don't really get to look under the hood.

---

13   Admittedly these difficulties are mainly a result of changes to the way that the Bank of England released the data. In July 2008 the Bank of England reclassified £14 billion of interest-bearing assets into non-interest-bearing ones. Previously the demand deposit section could be taken from the following series, 'Monthly amounts of UK residents banks (inc. Central Bank) sterling non-interest bearing deposits (inc. transit and suspense) from private sector' (LPMAUYA). But following the decision to lump £14 billion of assets into this measure it is no longer appropriate. As a result of this, in order to calculate the AMS an adjustment is required that is of a magnitude similar to the largest single component. I do not doubt that there is a valid reason for this. However, it makes the series hard to replicate and therefore reduces the validity.

14   http://blogs.forbes.com/michaelpollaro/austrian-money-supply/ (accessed 24 August 2016).

The TMS has problems with data availability and the fact that it includes savings. The AMS has a UK measure and is professionally maintained, but contains arbitrary adjustments, only includes retail (and not wholesale) deposits, and includes government deposits at the central banks. Since neither TMS nor AMS provide a dependable and publicly available measure for the UK, this paper attempts to provide one. I call it MA and publish it through Kaleidic Economics.[15]

MA is grounded in the definition of money's primary function as a medium of exchange. Conceptually, the closest of the measures discussed above would be White (1992). Crucially the ability to redeem an asset at par and on demand is *not* part of this definition because really these attributes relate to liquidity, not moneyness. If something can be exchanged *for* money, it cannot actually *be* money. Thus the ease with which an asset can be liquidated is not our concern – our focus is on assets that are already money.

In terms of justifying some of the decisions regarding what to include, it is worth commenting on three things in particular: savings accounts, money market mutual funds (MMMFs) and government deposits.

---

15 The notation is chosen to fit into the traditional UK distinction between M0 (narrow money) and M4 (broad money). The replacement of M0 with 'Notes and Coin' and the switch from M4 to M4x undermines this label, but the use of an 'M' to signal a money supply measure is fairly well established. It originates from Rothbard (1978), who uses *Ma*, where the '*a*' denotes 'Austrian'. In addition it avoids the mistaken hubris of labelling anything 'true' or 'actual'. It is published at http://www.kaleidic.org/data/.

- *Savings accounts*

  MA has important differences from other Austrian measures, both in the choice of series and the methods. Unlike the TMS I do *not* include savings accounts. Salerno's reasons for doing so are that 'the dollars accumulated ... are effectively withdrawable on demand ... [and] at all times transferable, dollar for dollar, into "transactions accounts"' (Salerno 1987: 3). However, they are not transferable *to other market participants*. Although people can draw a cheque on a savings account, to meet that obligation they must liquidate part of their savings by transferring assets into a chequing account. The savings account does not act as a final payment on goods and services. When financial innovation results in a savings account that can be drawn upon directly, this would become de facto demand deposits.

- *Money market mutual funds (MMMFs)*

  MMMFs are a form of investment that has a fluctuating price, and thus are not redeemable at par. If an investor wishes to liquidate an MMMF, they must instruct a fund manager to sell a portion of their holdings and then transfer the proceeds. These proceeds will fluctuate according to market conditions. Admittedly very few MMMFs 'break the buck' and investors have a reasonable expectation of redeeming them for par value. However, this is a necessary but not sufficient factor. Shostak (2000) raises the issue that MMMFs can be withdrawn on demand, but as Salerno (1987) points out 'they are neither instantly redeemable, par value claims to cash, nor final means of payment in exchange' – and thus not part of the money supply. In addition to this, retail market money funds are clearly not part of the money supply since short-term debt (e.g. government bonds or commercial paper) is not routinely used as a medium of exchange.

As White (1992) argues, MMMFs are a medium of exchange, but not a (sufficiently) generally accepted one. Despite being able to draw cheques (in some cases), users are not exchanging a claim on the actual portfolio. Rather, they are exchanging an inside-money claim against the bank. Since the second party does not obtain what the first party relinquishes, it is not money in our sense.

- *Government deposits*
  Both the TMS and AMS argue that government deposits should be incorporated into a measure of the money supply. According to Salerno (1987: 5), we are interested in 'the total stock of money owned by *all* economic agents' (emphasis in original), and therefore even when money is transferred from private to public accounts it is still part of the money supply: 'in reality, however, the money is now available for government expenditure, meaning that money held in government deposits should be part of the definition of money' (Shostak 2000). However, there is an inherent difficulty in counting the monopoly issuers' own holdings of a currency. The problem is that much of the government-held deposits

will consist of newly created money, or soon-to-be-retired money, and this would not be in circulation.[16] It is tempting to argue that this simply brings us back to the issue of subjectivism and whether an asset is being 'hoarded'. But the holdings of the issuer of a fiat currency have no economic significance.[17] It doesn't make sense to include freshly minted coins that sit in a government warehouse, and the same principle applies to government holdings of currency at the central banks.

When attempting to identify the money supply, there is an obvious trade-off between simplicity and accuracy. To some extent this is part of choosing between the top-down approach (looking at the Bankstats tables), and a bottom-up approach (looking for each individual series in the Statistical Interactive Database). The former is quicker and easier. The latter is more suitable to customisation.

The method of compiling MA has undergone several iterations. I released a co-authored working paper on the Social Science Research Network (SSRN) in June 2009, which was revised in March 2010 (see Evans and Baxendale 2010).[18] I

---

16 This is why many measures do not include government holdings of coin, but there seems to be an inconsistency when measures such as the TMS include Federal holdings of *notes* but exclude Federal holdings of *coin*.

17 I came to this view following an enlightening conversation with Jeffrey Rogers Hummel in the back of a minibus in Guatemala.

18 This was based on the following items: notes and coin; non-interest-bearing sight deposits; interest-bearing sight deposits; mutual institutions' instant access deposits.

then made significant revisions in July 2011 and published it through Kaleidic Economics.[19] In January 2012 the data were taken from a different source (Kaleidic Economics 2012), and then in July 2014 I stopped including the deposits of monetary and financial institutions (MFIs).[20] The aim has been simplicity. There will always be a gap between the definition and identification of the series, but important criteria are that series are publicly available, mutually compatible, and widely regarded as being legitimate. MA satisfies these criteria.[21] It is defined as follows:[22]

MA = Cash + Demand deposits

---

19 The items were: notes and coin; non-interest-bearing deposits; interest-bearing sight deposits; MFI sterling deposits from the public sector; and MFI sterling deposits from non-residents. The first six series were different on account of using raw (not seasonally adjusted) data. Due to a lack of data the last two were taken from Table B2.1, which unfortunately combines currency, deposits and money market instruments.

20 This is because they are interbank liabilities and therefore don't affect the spendable demand liabilities of the economy. In other words they do not constitute an increase in the money supply. I am grateful to Sean Corrigan for stressing this point (see Kaleidic Economics 2014). I originally labelled this MAex while I thought through the difference with MA, but now treat MA as not including MFI deposits.

21 Furthermore, given the lack of a reliable 'money of zero maturity' (MZM) measure for the UK, the subtleties of an Austrian approach are less important. MZM is a similar measure to MA in that it focuses on liquid assets (Carlson and Keen 1996; Teles and Zhou 2005). However, the Fed includes MMMFs in its measure of MZM, making it slightly broader than MA.

22 The benefit of Table A6.1 is that it splits up non-interest-bearing and interest-bearing deposits, but for the purposes of MA whether the account pays interest or not does not matter. Unfortunately, Table A6.1 is also seasonally adjusted.

Full details, including series codes, are provided in Table 2 at the end of this chapter (pages 44–45).[23] Conveniently, since January 2010, the items identified as 'cash' can be found in Table A1.1.1 'Notes and coin and reserve balances' and all of the items identified as 'demand deposits' can be found in Table B1.4 'Monetary financial institutions (excluding central bank) balance sheet'. The majority of the series used for backdating start in April 1990, so this is as far back as MA goes. It is accurate as of August 2016.

Figure 3 shows the MA stock from April 1990 to June 2016.

Figure 3   MA stock, 1990–2016 (£million)

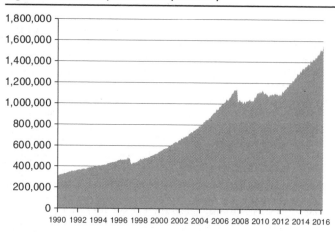

23 I am grateful to Peter Stellios for helping me to find comparable series that go back to 1990.

Figure 4 shows the year-on-year growth rate for MA for the entire range of data available.[24]

Figure 4   MA growth, 1991–2016 (year-on-year % change)

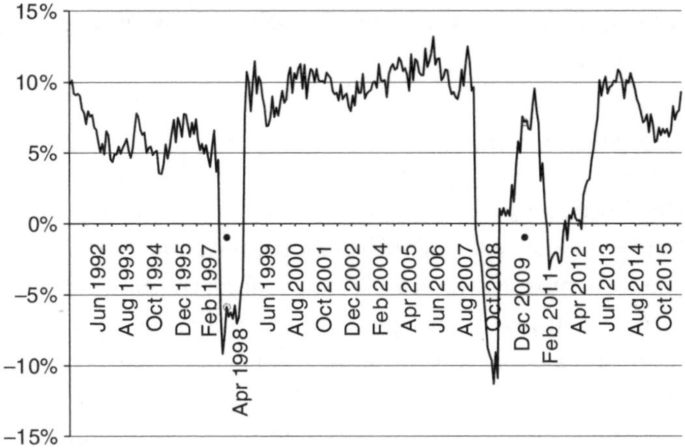

The Goldilocks measure

The convention of taking a narrow/broad approach to monetary aggregates is appealing since it captures the whole range of the monetary transmission mechanism, from the base money that is created by the Bank of England to the additional demand deposits and accounts that are generated through fractional reserve banking. The main problem, though, is that there is a trade-off involved in both. Narrow money is easy to measure, but does not

---

24 The black dots indicate a change in the series.

have a clear link to what is happening in the wider, real economy. Broad money is more likely to capture economic activity, but is susceptible to lags and dependent on the transmission mechanism working in a stable manner.[25] Indeed, we can look in turn at problems with narrow and broad measures.

Narrow is too narrow

One important limitation in focusing purely on Notes and Coin is what types of transaction they fund.[26] Although accurate numbers are impossible to find, the conventional view is that less than 1 per cent of total transactions are paid for with cash, and around 50 per cent of cash is held in the informal economy (Congdon 2007).[27] Table 1 shows the monthly average amount outstanding of Notes and Coin as of 31 December 2010.[28]

---

25 One argument may be that this is what happened during the credit crunch – the transmission mechanism broke down, with large spreads arising between the Bank rate and the interbank rate (i.e. LIBOR). QE can be seen as an attempt by the Bank of England to restore control over the broad money supply. However, when QE was adopted this generated a surge in bank reserves, but since they did not seem to find their way into the real money balances of consumers they had a questionable impact on short-term inflation and output.

26 Note that we are interested in total 'transactions' here rather than components of GDP.

27 Indeed if anything this casts doubt over whether bank notes should be considered 'money' as we've defined it.

28 Elsewhere in this book we use measure Notes and Coin with series LP-MAVAA (not seasonally adjusted), which provides a total of £59,641 million.

Table 1   Notes and Coin breakdown

	£m
Household sector (LPMVYWO)	48,011
Other financial corporations (LPMB75C)	83
Private non-financial corporations (LPMB76C)	4,263
Total	52,357

If we assume there are about 53 million adults in the UK,[29] this implies an average cash holding of £906 per person. As Congdon (2007) concludes, even if we factor in private businesses that are cash intensive, this implies that a lot of cash is held in the informal economy.

Conceptually, MA resembles other narrow measures of the money supply, such as non-interest-bearing M1 and MZM. M1 is undermined by the fact that demand deposits typically pay interest. In addition, sweep provisions are a means for checking accounts to evade reserve requirements, but they result in M1 failing to pick up on a sizeable amount of money held in a demand deposit account. A further problem is explained by McLeay et al. (2014: 9):

> During the financial crisis when interest rates fell close to zero, the growth of non-interest bearing M1 picked up markedly as the relative cost of holding a non-interest bearing deposit fell sharply compared to an interest-bearing one. Focusing on M1 would have given a

29 For population statistics see https://www.ons.gov.uk/peoplepopulation andcommunity/populationandmigration/populationestimates/articles/ overviewoftheukpopulation/july2017/pdf.

misleading signal about the growth of nominal spending in the economy.

Money of zero maturity (MZM) is defined as 'notes and coin plus all sight deposits held by the non-bank private sector' (ibid.: 10). It isn't published by the Bank of England, although they do say it 'can be constructed from published components' (ibid.). MA is not intended to be an estimate of MZM but there are likely to be close similarities.

There is also the issue of substitutability. In the US the statistical relationship between M1 and national income began to fail in the 1980s as people increasingly switched between savings and NOW (negotiable order of with-drawal) accounts,[30] and in 1993 Alan Greenspan said, 'M2 has been downgraded as a reliable indicator of financial conditions in the economy, and no single variable has yet been identified to take its place'.[31] This is partly why many economists see little middle ground between M0 and M4.

Broad is too broad

So 'narrow' money might be considered *too* narrow, but that doesn't make 'broad' money appropriate. M4 is the conventional measure of broad money and includes all deposits (sight deposits plus time deposits) held with non-financial companies and non-bank financial compa-nies (McLeay et al. 2014: 9). As already discussed, there

---

30 The former are part of M2 whereas the latter are also in M1.

31 Comments by Alan Greenspan in a Congressional Testimony, July 1993.

are question marks relating to the robustness of M4 due to sporadic reclassifications. When non-banks get reclassified as banks this will be revealed in broad money measures despite there being no change to actual lending.[32] The key issue here remains the definition of money, which Congdon defines as 'assets with a given nominal value' (Congdon 2007: 9). However, this conflicts with *our* prior definition, which requires that the asset be used in exchange. Even if the nominal value is fixed, if an underlying asset needs to be sold in order to cash it in, it isn't money in our sense. Bonds tend to have a given nominal value, but they are not money because they are not a generally accepted medium of exchange.

The concept of monetary disequilibrium shows how the real balance effect works: if 'real broad money balances differ from their desired levels in the aggregate, equilibrium can be restored only by changes in demand, output, employment and the price level' (Congdon 1995: 25).[33] However, there is a balance between incorporating any assets that play a role in the transmission mechanism and *money*.

Some argue that there is no real middle ground on the spectrum of liquidity. For example, a popular economics textbook says, 'Once we leave cash in circulation, the first sensible place to stop is M4' (Begg et al. 2008: 442). However, a tight definition of money does allow a non-arbitrary

---

32 'Non-banks' comprise households, companies and financial institutions.

33 For Congdon the transmission mechanism is basically: broad money → asset prices → national expenditure/income (Congdon 2007: 1).

balance, and this middle ground receives empirical validation.

Figure 5   Monetary aggregates, September 2014 (£million)

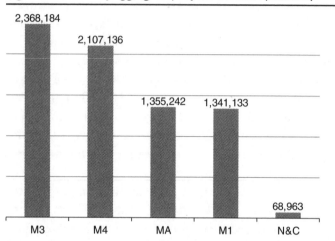

Figure 5 shows the stock of various standard monetary aggregates, as of September 2014. MA is 57 per cent of M3, 20 times the size of Notes and Coin, and slightly larger than M1. Figure 6 shows how MA compares to these money supply measures over time.[34]

This shows that before the financial crisis MA fell in between M1 and M4. A key thing to note is that MA begins to contract a lot sooner, and more noticeably, than any other aggregate (indeed M1 was rising). One of the criticisms of

---

34 The series codes used are VWYZ (M3), AUYN (M4), VWYT (M1) and AVAB (Notes and Coin).

narrow money supply measures is that flights to safety will show as a monetary impetus and mask a collapse in the money multiplier. MA is broad enough to avoid this problem, but not so broad that the scale makes sudden changes unnoticeable. Also note that M4 and M3 clearly show the artificial stimulus of QE in the period March 2009 to February 2010.[35]

Figure 6   Monetary aggregates, 2004–16 (£million)

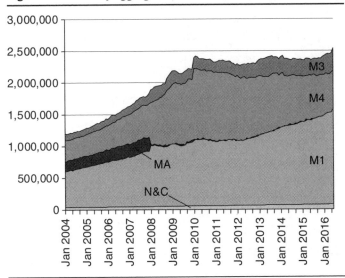

Figure 7 compares MA with M3. The latter has been a useful measure of the broad money supply during the financial crisis, showing a slowdown in the growth of money and a contraction from October 2010 to November

35 Due to data comparability issues I am using M4 despite the criticisms made earlier in the book.

2012. However, MA clearly offers more predictive power with the sharp contraction from January 2008 to December 2008, a second one from January 2011 to June 2011, and stronger growth since 2013.

Figure 7   M3 and MA, 2004–16 (year-on-year growth rates)

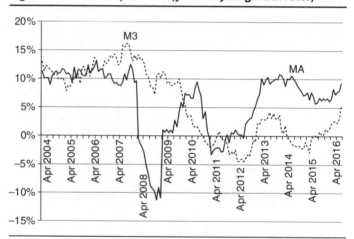

Divisia money

Divisia measures are named after the (ever less) neglected French economist, François Divisia. He published a series of articles in the 1920s, in the French journal *Revue d'économie Politique*. They have been adopted and advocated by William Barnett,[36] who uses them as the centrepiece of

---

36 See Barnett (1980) for the seminal avocation and Barnett (2012) for a highly readable overview.

a monetary theory that posits that the business cycle is caused by poor quality central bank data. He argues that both economic theory and best practice measurement is inconsistent with indices that are based on addition, without weighting the various components. Because it includes asset classes that are not highly liquid, Divisia money can be viewed as a broad aggregate. However, crucially, it is weighted based on the extent to which the asset performs monetary services. Interest rates are used to estimate the opportunity cost of holding liquid assets, and it is assumed that more liquid assets provide greater money services. Hence the money supply becomes a utility function where narrower components contribute a greater share. The easier it is for money to be used in transactions, the greater the weight (or 'value share').

Belongia (1996) has shown that the impact of the money supply on economic activity depends critically on the choice of monetary aggregate being used, and replicates studies using Divisia measures to demonstrate their superiority. Belongia and Ireland (2010) utilise a Divisia measure within a contemporary New Keynesian model and demonstrate its superiority over a simple sum alternative. Hendrickson (2013) replicates important previous articles, and finds a stable money demand function if Divisia measures are used. He also shows evidence that Divisia measures have causal impact on output and prices, supporting Barnett's (2012) claim that the apparent breakdown in the usefulness of monetary aggregates is due to measurement error. Belongia and Ireland (2014) cast doubt on the prevalence of macroeconomic models that focus on interest rates, rather than money, and show that money regains its predictive power once Divisia measures are used. While the Federal Reserve and the Bank of England provide Divisia estimates for the US and UK respectively, no such official measure exists for the Eurozone. Darvas (2014) is an attempt to provide one, and also utilises an SVAR model to find that Divisia money shocks have a statistically significant impact on important macroeconomic indicators. Finally, Brown (2013) uses a bi-variate VAR test for Granger-causality and finds evidence that Divisia monetary aggregates cause nominal spending. As alluded to previously, if policymakers look at the wrong measures, this can hamper policy decisions. And Barnett and Chauvet (2011) argue that bad monetary measures have indeed led policymakers astray.

As Hancock (2005) points out, Divisia measures rest on two important assumptions. Firstly, that the more liquid the asset, the more useful it is for transaction purposes. And secondly, that the more liquid the asset, the lower the amount of interest paid.[37] However, there is no a priori link between the amount of interest being paid on an asset and its usefulness as a medium of exchange. For example, many internet-based transactions are easier to use with a debit card than cash. Yet current accounts pay higher interest than currency.

According to Barnett (2012: 118), demand deposits are 'joint products' that provide multiple services: 'two

---

37 Similarly, 'it is assumed that relatively illiquid deposits are less likely to be used for transaction purposes than highly liquid financial assets in the money supply and that higher interest rates are paid on the less liquid money components' (IMF 2008, cited in Barnett 2012: 65).

motives exist for holding money: monetary services, such as liquidity, and investment return, such as interest'. But there's a slippery slope here given that in practice all financial products provide multiple services. And it is problematic to attempt to empirically observe or infer motivations. Barnett (2012) uses the example of a Ferrari. It is a joint product in the sense that it is a means of transportation and also a source of recreation. But it is difficult to identify what the cost of a car would be purely for transportation services and then deduce a premium that people pay for recreation use. Subjectivism implies that once we have a non-arbitrary definition of a car (e.g. a four-wheeled passenger vehicle that can be operated on ordinary roads) we cannot impute what proportion of the total stock of cars delivers more value as a transportation device. Friedman and Schwartz (1970: 116) try to get around this by saying that we can empirically determine the values being attributed to each component, but this only holds if prices are in equilibrium. If we suspect that we live in a world of disequilibrium, then these data are out of reach.

As previously mentioned, we can define money as the generally accepted medium of exchange and view other uses of money as being derivatives of this. According to the IMF (2008: 183–84), 'a Divisia money formulation takes account of the trade-off between the medium-of-exchange and store-of-value functions of holding money components'. But a subjectivist approach denies that this is a trade-off. They are related and part and parcel of what constitutes money.

Hancock (2005: 40) also details four difficulties in terms of compilation. These are:

[T]he choice of the benchmark asset and rate; the interest rates paid on individual Divisia components; the appropriate level of aggregation; and problems of 'break-adjustments'.

These 'difficulties' are highlighted by revealing that prior to 2005 the benchmark rate was based on three-month Local Government (LG) bills, and a totally arbitrary adjustment of 200 basis points to ensure that there weren't any components of M4 that had a lower return (Hancock 2005: 40)! We can see UK Divisia in Figure 8.

Figure 8   Divisia money, 2000–2016 (year-on-year % growth)

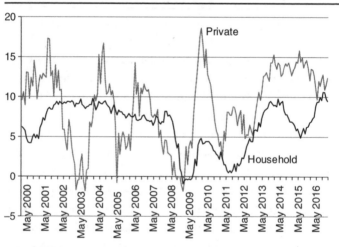

Household spending seems a lot more informative than private non-financial corporations. Note that QE began in March 2009, was increased in August 2009 and then again in November 2009. A further round occurred in October–May 2011, and again in July 2012.

Divisia measures have much in common with Austrian measures. Ultimately, they are an attempt to measure the moneyness spectrum mentioned by Hutt (1956) and Horwitz (1990, 1994). By focusing on the use of money in exchange they rightly incorporate interest-paying asset classes.

Recollect our definition of MA:

$$MA = C + D.$$

We can incorporate a Divisia approach by amending it thus:

$$MA_D = Ca + bD.$$

Like any additive monetary aggregate, it is essentially a binary Divisia measure. The coefficients a and b both equal 1, and the coefficients for any number of asset classes not listed are 0.[38] We could attempt to tweak these weights (or value shares) such that currency is weighted more heavily than deposits. But this method is not based on the legitimate assumption that deposits earn higher interest, but the more dubious claim that this makes deposits less useful for transaction purchases than currency. A contactless debit card means that £1,000 in my current account is far more marketable than my Vegemite jar full of pennies. According to Horwitz (1990), 'Even a demand deposit is not

---

38 Therefore, as an anonymous referee points out, $MA_D = Ca + bD + cZ$, where Z refers to all other assets and $c = 0$.

quite as available as currency or coin is – some places will not accept checks'. True, but who uses cheques these days? Some (online) places do not accept cash. Any attempt to change the coefficients enters problematic territory.

According to Lars Christensen (2013), the advantage of Divisia measures is that they reveal a 'major movement of money in the UK economy – from less liquid time deposits to more liquid readably available short-term deposits'. This is because 'a shift in cash holdings from time deposits to short-term deposits will cause an increase in the Divisia Money supply' (ibid.). But note that the same applies to MA. The problem with Divisia is that the greater the extent to which it correlates with and predicts nominal spending, the less useful it becomes as a monetary indicator. Similarly, M4 is adjusted when it is 'likely to provide a measure of money more closely related to nominal spending' (Janssen 2009: 1). The broadest possible definition of money will, ultimately, deliver nominal GDP (NGDP). If statistical relationships are the goal, that's where you end up. By contrast a tight theoretical definition may not match NGDP quite so nicely, but it could have more predictive ability (in terms of the extent to which it is not merely an attempt to measure NGDP).

Conclusion

Financial innovation (such as payments technology) and changes in consumer preferences will impact how we define the money supply, and all measures are subject to the idiosyncrasies of official central bank data. Most economists believe that at various times the insights of monetary aggregates have broken down. Others, such as Barnett (2012), argue that the monetary aggregates have been stable if measured correctly. But they needn't be stable to be useful. As Hamilton (2006) has said:

> [U]nless the fraction of assets held as M2 is continually subject to new shocks, once the shift has occurred, we would thereafter expect to see the correlation between the growth rates resume.

This chapter defines and identifies a pioneering measure of the money supply (MA), based on an Austrian-school approach. The intention has not been to perform a robust statistical test of this measure vis-à-vis existing alternatives, but to focus on its theoretical sturdiness. It finds a middle ground between narrow and broad money, avoiding some of the problems with the conventional data. A cursory look suggests that it warrants further attention. It is presented to serve as a complement to, rather than a substitute for, existing measures. As policymakers and commentators increasingly turn their attention to money growth, a discussion about the definition of money and an appraisal of the strengths and weaknesses of different measures should become mandatory. The money supply – accurately defined and identified – plays a crucial role in understanding the path of the real economy over the shorter term, as well as being the root cause of price inflation. Money matters.

Table 2   MA data series and backdating methods

	Apr 1990 to Aug 1997	Sep 1997 to Jan 2008
Notes and Coin	LPMAVAA Monthly average amount outstanding of total sterling notes and coin in circulation, excluding backing assets for commercial banknote issue in Scotland and Northern Ireland total (in sterling millions) not seasonally adjusted.	
UK Public sector	RPMATFD Monthly amounts outstanding of UK resident banks' inc. BoE Banking Department (monthly balance sheet reporters) sterling sight deposits from public sector (in sterling millions) not seasonally adjusted.	RPMTBFD Monthly amounts outstanding of UK resident banks' (excl. Central Bank) sterling sight deposits from public sector (in sterling millions) not seasonally adjusted.
UK Private sector	RPMATFE Monthly amounts outstanding of UK resident banks' inc. BoE Banking Department (monthly balance sheet reporters) sterling sight deposits from private sector (in sterling millions) not seasonally adjusted.	RPMTBFE Monthly amounts outstanding of UK resident banks' (excl. Central Bank) sterling sight deposits from private sector (in sterling millions) not seasonally adjusted.
	LPMB85E Monthly amounts outstanding of building societies' sterling sight deposits from private sector (in sterling millions) not seasonally adjusted.	
Non-residents	RPMATFF Monthly amounts outstanding of UK resident banks' inc. BoE Banking Department (monthly balance sheet reporters) sterling sight deposits from non-residents (in sterling millions) not seasonally adjusted.	RPMTBFF Monthly amounts outstanding of UK resident banks' (excl. Central Bank) sterling sight deposits from non-residents (in sterling millions) not seasonally adjusted.

Table 2 (*cont.*)

	Jan 2008 to Dec 2009	*Jan 2010 to Dec 2013*
Notes and Coin	LPMAVAA Monthly average amount outstanding of total sterling notes and coin in circulation, excluding backing assets for commercial banknote issue in Scotland and Northern Ireland total (in sterling millions) not seasonally adjusted.	
UK Public sector	LPMB84E Monthly amounts outstanding of building societies' sterling sight deposits from public sector (in sterling millions) not seasonally adjusted.	RPMB3MM Monthly amounts outstanding of UK resident monetary financial institutions' (excl. Central Bank) sterling sight deposits from public sector (in sterling millions) not seasonally adjusted.
UK Private sector	LPMB85E Monthly amounts outstanding of building societies' sterling sight deposits from private sector (in sterling millions) not seasonally adjusted.	RPMB3NM Monthly amounts outstanding of UK resident monetary financial institutions' (excl. Central Bank) sterling sight deposits from private sector (in sterling millions) not seasonally adjusted.
Non-residents	LPMB86E Monthly amounts outstanding of building societies' sterling sight deposits from non-residents (in sterling millions) not seasonally adjusted.	RPMB3OM Monthly amounts outstanding of UK resident monetary financial institutions' (excl. Central Bank) sterling sight deposits from non-residents (in sterling millions) not seasonally adjusted.

3 V: VELOCITY SHOCKS, REGIME UNCERTAINTY AND THE CENTRAL BANK

Summary of key points

- It is possible that emergency monetary policy *generates* the increase in the demand for money that it professes to be attempting to accommodate.
- The public's demand to hold money can have important macroeconomic effects, but a subjectivist approach makes it difficult to model.
- Central bankers are right to alter monetary policy in light of such changes (i.e. velocity shocks), but they also need to recognise the potential for their own actions to be the cause of such shocks.
- In particular, central banks are 'big players' who can weaken confidence by generating regime uncertainty, and this played a major role in the 2008 financial crisis.
- Although it was adopted with the intention of reducing uncertainty, forward guidance can also increase uncertainty.
- While this increased attention to uncertainty by economists should be welcomed, we should also be wary of attempts to measure it.

Without warning, the Fed and the Treasury changed TBTF [too big to fail] in October [2008], allowing Lehman Brothers to fail. That policy did not continue. Days later, the Fed bailed out American International Group by investing $180 billion in the failing company. These shifts in policy greatly increased uncertainty about what would happen next. Financial firms and others responded by greatly increasing the demand for cash. The Fed responded appropriately by acting as lender of last resort to financial markets at home and abroad by increasing the supply of cash assets.

Meltzer (2012: 256)

Introduction

Central bankers are inclined to regard the economic shocks that they have to respond to as being largely exogenous. The purpose of this chapter is to suggest that one particular type of demand shock – a fall in velocity – can be an unintended consequence of central bank actions. To do this, I will draw together several important economic concepts. These are the demand for money, supplier-induced demand (SID) and regime uncertainty. Many economists – and monetarists in particular – maintain that the money supply is the chief cause of disturbances to nominal income. Milton Friedman famously argued that the demand for money was reasonably stable, because usually any change in factors that influence it have been caused by prior changes in the money supply.[1] If large changes in velocity were indeed being caused by unstable monetary policy, then velocity could be made stable with a commitment to constant money growth (see Hummel 2011: 489). However, money growth is not the only way that central banks conduct monetary policy, and velocity shocks can arise from a number of sources. While Keynesians tend to explain such autonomous changes in velocity as the result of 'animal spirits', we will see how regime uncertainty can provide a more convincing explanation. Crucially, it attributes such shocks to central bank error. According to the equation of exchange, aggregate demand shocks arise either through M (i.e. a monetary contraction) or V (i.e. a fall in velocity). The point here is to bridge these two claims by arguing that non-monetary influences of the central bank (through its authority as a big player) can hinder confidence and force policymakers into a difficult decision about the optimal monetary response.

To understand the concept of velocity (the rate at which people spend money), the first section looks at the theory behind the demand for money, with specific reference to the subjectivist approach of the Austrian school. Rather than relegate it to a mere residual within the equation of exchange, we will look at its function as a unifying factor. Indeed we can see how velocity shocks affected the 2008 financial crisis. In the second section, the concept of

---

1   It is tempting to oversimplify a prolific scholar who modified his views over time. For example, Friedman (1956: 16) made it clear that velocity isn't stable per se, rather it has a predictable relationship with a small number of variables.

'supplier-induced demand' will be used to discuss central banks' culpability in creating a reduction in aggregate demand. The third section of this chapter looks more closely at the channel through which this negative velocity shock occurred. The concept of regime uncertainty will be defined and attempts to measure it will be critically discussed.

The demand for money

In a seminal contribution David Laidler (1969) grappled with the question of whether or not the theory of demand that is used to study all goods and services can be used when it comes to money. He recognised that economists tend not to be interested in the precise nature of a utility function – it is enough to say that a good or service delivers consumer satisfaction. However, he casts doubt on whether this applies to money (Laidler 1969: 51):

> It is not something that is physically consumed, nor does it, like other consumer durable goods, seem to yield a flow of services that give psychological satisfaction to an individual.

But perhaps the problem is not with the nature of money, but with the theory of demand being used – and, in particular, its lack of subjectivism. After all, the utility that we gain from consuming physical goods arises from the fact that it satisfies an unmet need. Thus it's not really the apple that we value per se, but the alleviation of hunger.

A product is simply a vehicle for want-satisfaction. Laidler acknowledges that money *can* be interest bearing, in which case he seems to accept that a service is being provided. But he goes on to say that 'There are many instances of money yielding no interest and being held nevertheless. It may look, then, as if utility theory cannot be used as a direct explanation as to why money is held, so that the demand for it must be treated as a special case' (ibid.).

Laidler lists two characteristics that demonstrate how money is unique. Firstly, it facilitates exchange, and, secondly, its exchange value is reasonably predictable. It is important to note that both of these characteristics stem from the fact that we live in a world of uncertainty.[2] We demand to hold the medium of exchange because it reduces the transaction costs of having to convert interest-bearing assets to money whenever we want to engage in market exchange. And if there is uncertainty regarding future asset prices, keeping wealth as cash may help avoid taking a loss. Following Patinkin (1965: 117), we can distinguish between transactions demand (stemming from uncertainty over the timing of payments and receipts); and precautionary demand (regarding the future value of bonds). But he makes clear that both of these stem from uncertainty.[3]

---

2   Although Luther (2016) presents reasons why money may emerge for reasons other than uncertainty.

3   Uncertainty is a necessary consequence of the fact that action takes place over time. This is a further reason why it is difficult to split up various 'motives' for the demand for money: '*all* motives for holding money require that it be held for a positive time interval before being spent: there is no reason to use money (as opposed to barter) if it is to be received for goods and then instantaneously exchanged for other goods' (Lucas 1972: 107).

Laidler (1969: 52) continued to accept that 'these two characteristics, which are usually collectively called *liquidity*, are not the exclusive property of money. Other assets also possess them in varying degrees'. So having failed to make the case for why utility theory does not apply to money, all he can do is define money as being especially liquid. A subjectivist approach to money leads to a clearer, albeit less empirically visible characterisation. To be fair, Laidler accepts that money might provide 'important services' (ibid.: 53)[4] and concedes that 'these various models could be regarded as all forming part of one general theory of the demand for money' (ibid.: 54). However, he resorts to the positivist claim that the grounding of the theory of the demand for money is secondary to the predictive power it generates (ibid.: 53) and that treating each theory as a separate hypothesis will lead to a more parsimonious result. By contrast, the approach taken here has no inhibitions about the claim that money provides 'a stream of subjective utility' (Horwitz 1990: 469), and intends to view competing theories as complements rather than substitutes.[5]

Following Laidler, we can use the equation of exchange as the starting point to consider the conventional ways of

---

4   Although he continues by saying 'even if such services are not of the kind that yield psychological satisfaction' (ibid.: 53). But it's hard to consider any form of satisfaction that isn't 'psychological'.

5   As Lucas points out, it isn't controversial to claim that holding money provides utility services, 'There is also the question of whether money "yields utility." Certainly the answer in this context is yes, in the sense that if one imposes on an individual the constraint that he cannot hold cash, his utility under an optimal policy is lower than it will be if this constraint is removed' (Lucas 1972: 107).

viewing the demand for money. The Fisherian version is concerned with the volume of transactions, T, and therefore velocity is the transactions velocity:

$$M\bar{V}_T = P\bar{T}.$$

If our attention is on the use of money as a medium of exchange, the institutions of exchange (such as payments systems) will be a crucial factor in the demand to hold it. But because they are likely to be relatively stable, it is conventional to assume that V and T are also relatively stable. As Laidler (1969: 58) says, 'over short time periods, there is little scope for the variation in the amount of money demanded relative to the volume of transactions being conducted'. Hence, 'the transactions approach to monetary theory ... tends to lead to the hypothesis that the demand for money is a constant proportion of the level of transactions, which in turn bears a constant relationship to the level of national income' (ibid.).[6]

The Cambridge approach is more concerned with individual decision-making, and can be summarised as follows:

$$M_d = kP\bar{Y}.$$

Instead of looking at the volume of all transactions (i.e. how much cash you need to make your expected purchases), the demand for money is treated as a proportion of income (i.e. how much of your income you wish to hold as

---

6   Having said this, trends in vertical integration will impact transactions velocity, and as Laidler (1969: 58) concedes (in a footnote), 'this whole line of reasoning ... overlooks the large and rapid fluctuations that can take place in the volume of transactions conducted in financial markets'.

cash). This is a broader question and draws in the reasons why people may wish to hold on to money during certain economic situations. It is tempting to make an assumption that T/Y is constant, and define $k = 1/V$.[7] In this case we can treat the two equations as being the same (see Mankiw 2002: 88; Evans and Thorpe 2013). However, Laidler (1969: 62) points out that there is an important difference. While the transactions velocity can be treated as being constant over short time periods, 'not so with the Cambridge economists with their emphasis on the rate of interest and expectations, for these are variables one can expect to vary significantly over quite short periods'.

Due to uncertainty, it would be imprudent to only carry the bare minimum amount of money needed to fund expected transactions, and so we can also think about a 'precautionary' motive (although it isn't clear the extent to which we can differentiate between the two given that if there were no uncertainty we may not need money at all). Keynes then identified the price of bonds (i.e. the interest rate) as the opportunity cost of holding money and a key source of uncertainty that people face. Hence, interest rates are inversely related to the demand for money. Taking this view, it becomes even more tempting to treat the transactions demand and speculative demand as two competing theories, with one driven by an automatic response to slow changing institutional trends, and the other characterised by erratic people responding quickly to changes in interest rates. We can also view Friedman's main contribution in

---

7   See Selgin (1988: 67) for how this applies to inside money.

terms of adopting an empirical agenda, incorporating 'the present value of labour income' (ibid.: 70) – i.e. wealth.[8]

Following Horwitz (1994), we can view a subjectivist approach as having two components. Firstly, it requires that we take a broad view of the substitutes for money. He argues that 'the cost of holding money is the expected utility sacrificed from the next best alternative use' (ibid.: 465) and discusses how the Keynesian emphasis on 'speculative' demand for money concentrates on the relationship between the demand and supply of money, and the demand and supply of bonds.[9] But bonds are not the only substitute for money.[10] Monetarists attempted to broaden the range of assets that were deemed to be substitutes for money, but according to Horwitz, 'Friedman did not spread his substitutes wide enough ... any and all utility-yielding assets are substitutes for money. The demand for money will be affected by changes in the utility yields

---

8 'Wealth should probably be the scale variable in the demand for money function' (Goodhart 2007).

9 This is why Keynesian models tend to place a greater emphasis on interest rates (i.e. the price of bonds) than the price level when looking at the impact of monetary disequilibrium.

10 Horwitz (1990: 467) says, 'when one models bonds as the only substitute for money, it will indeed be true that even small changes in the interest rate will affect the quantity demanded and that the Keynesian policy implications will follow'. But of course this doesn't mean that interest rates aren't important at all – a rise in interest rates can be expected to cause an increase in the demand for interest-bearing demand deposit accounts (relative to cash) and an increase in demand for bonds (relative to interest-bearing demand deposit accounts). According to Horwitz (ibid.: 464), accounts that focus on the trade-off between interest-bearing securities and 'money' (i.e. on the transaction costs of the former) neglect the more pertinent trade-off between holding financial assets and holding goods and services.

of all other goods not simply the flow of interest yields from bonds' (ibid.: 467).[11]

There is an array of factors that influence the demand for money, such as:

- the amount of nominal spending on transactions;
- wealth;
- the opportunity cost of holding money;
- uncertainty over future liquidity requirements.

Each is important in different situations, and depending on different institutional structures.

The typical literature is a debate about how to model the utility function. Hence, as Howden (2013: 26) asks, 'Is the velocity of circulation determined or at least influenced by the nominal interest rate (Laidler 1989), real interest rate (Friedman 1956), the expected inflation rate (Laidler 1991), or is it a passively determined variable (Keynes 1923)?' This has the danger of drawing attention away from appreciating the multifaceted way in which people choose their money holdings, and the impact of interest rates on individual choice. Furthermore, the interest rate is not the opportunity cost of money; it is part of the opportunity cost of anything other than bonds (Hutt 1963). As Egger (1994: 135) says, '[the] reason for holding cash balances ... was just a combination of transaction costs and uncertainty

---

11 Similarly, White (1999: 111) provides a nice, simplified money demand relationship by saying that it is a positive function of the real volume of transactions (or indeed income, which may serve as a useful proxy) and a negative function of the opportunity cost of holding money.

about future prices ... [and] bears no necessary relation to the current level of interest'.[12]

The second facet to a subjectivist approach is the rooting of monetary equilibrium in individual choice. According to Horwitz (1994: 467), 'the Cambridge real-balance approach provides the essential insight that money holders wish to hold some desired level of real purchasing power'. Hence if there's an increase in the money supply such that people hold more cash balances than they desire, their demand for goods and services (relative to their demand for money) rises and they increase their spending. Inflation is simply the consequence of people returning to their desired cash balance. Therefore money can be understood using standard demand theory, in other words, 'The subjectivist approach can explain this as simply an application of marginal utility theory' (ibid.).

An important part of this subjectivist approach is to emphasise that the demand for money is based on the demand to *hold* money.[13] While it is true that money is demanded because it serves as the medium of exchange,

---

12 Artus (2015) argues that the breakdown between the money supply and prices since 2008 is because 'money demand is now no longer related to transactions and income, but corresponds to the portfolio choice of economic agents'. This could also serve as an argument in favour of giving more attention to financial asset prices and real estate prices in our measures of inflation and output (i.e. putting emphasis on measuring transactions rather than just the output of final goods). The real choice, however, is whether we should search for a more accurate utility function, or recognise that money demand is no easier to capture in an economic model than any other type of demand.

13 As Selgin (1988: 52) says, it is 'desire to *hold* money as part of a financial portfolio'.

and therefore people have an intention to use it at some point, when any good changes hands it is reflecting supply as much as demand. Selgin cites Cannan (1921), who said 'the demand which is important for our purposes is the demand for money, not to pay away again immediately, but to hold'. Splitting the demand for money into transaction or speculative 'motives' does not alter this. Indeed Friedman (1956: 14) argued that we can't split the demand for money up based on motives, or distinguish between 'active' or 'idle' use. The whole point of a medium of exchange is that it is ready for use, and the only difference between money that is 'in circulation' or 'idle' is the period of time in which it changes ownership. This point drives straight to the heart of Keynesian orthodoxy that finds relevance in the motivation that people have when holding cash balances and other liquid assets. It is misleading to deem cash balances 'idle' or bemoan 'hoarding' – the value of money, like the value of any other commodity, is subjective, and stems from its availability (Hutt 1956; Horwitz 1990).

There are several different ways to go about measuring the demand for money. The simplest is to take the equation of exchange, and solve for V:

$$V = (P + Y) - M$$

Figure 9 shows broad money velocity for the UK from 2007 to 2010.[14] Velocity is shown to decline in Q1 2008, and

---

14 I've used a measure of M4x (series code RPQB3DI) due to its availability as a quarterly measure, and NGDP growth (series code IHYO).

reaches a trough in Q1 2009. A fall in velocity constitutes a negative confidence shock.

Figure 9   Broad money velocity, 2007–10 (% change)

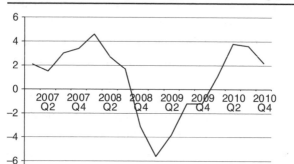

Obviously, a choice has to be made about which monetary aggregate to use, but another problem with this approach is that it treats the demand for money as a mere residual. This means that it also contains an error component and is only as strong as the measures of M, P and Y (see Friedman 1987; Howden 2013). This is a pity, because we should really see the demand for money as the unifying factor in the equation of exchange, since it grounds an apparent aggregate relationship in a theory of individual choice.

Soon after the financial crisis ended, economists (especially in America) began pointing to velocity as being an important part of the story. Without attempting to measure money per se, Beckworth (2011a) shows the ratio of liquid assets (such as money, MMAs and T-bills) to all household assets, arguing 'households and firms are still holding a disproportionate share of their assets in liquid form' (see also Beckworth 2011b). By September 2010 the ratio of total liquid assets to total assets was the highest it had been for over fifty years (Greenspan 2011: 167).[15] Beckworth (2011b) has pointed to evidence showing that the Federal Reserve recognised an increase in money demand in September 2011:

> M2 surged in July and August, as investors and asset managers sought the relative safety and liquidity of bank deposits and other assets that make up the M2 aggregate.

Crucially, he points out that this increase in M2 was not being driven by higher incomes, but by people's desire to hold a higher proportion of their income in a liquid form: 'the growth in savings is clearly not an increase in money demand from income growth. It is all about holding precautionary money balances' (ibid.). The way that it tends to be reported by central banks is that this spike is some kind of exogenous shock that is a result of outside factors and needs to be accommodated. It generates macroeconomic disturbances because an increase in the demand for money (people's desire to hold money) means a fall in velocity (the rate at which people spend it). And as per the equation of exchange, this constitutes a fall in aggregate demand and nominal income.

---

15 This neatly avoids the problem of defining money by looking at the composition of people's financial portfolios.

Beckworth (2013) lists several factors as contributing to the demand for money and money-like assets, such as the Great Recession, the euro zone debt crisis, concerns about the growth rate of China, and disputes about the debt ceiling debate. However, this does not mean that the central bank is not culpable for a demand for money-induced reduction in nominal spending:

> Through its control of the monetary base, the Fed can shape expectations of the future path of current-dollar or nominal spending. Thus, for every spike in broad money demand, the Fed could have responded in a systematic manner to prevent the spike from depressing both spending and interest rates.[16]

Regarding events in 2008, Beckworth points out a decline in the money multiplier, which he argues occurred as a result of a breakdown in financial intermediation, and the paying of interest on reserves. However, an increase in the monetary base failed to fully offset this. This was because, 'it seems that on balance it has been the fall in velocity (i.e. the increase in real money demand) that has driven the collapse in nominal spending' (Beckworth 2009). He argues that 'The decline in the velocity is presumably the result of an increase in real money demand created by the uncertainty surrounding the recession' (ibid.).

---

16 Hence, 'Given that we have a central bank – and this is not an endorsement of the Fed – its job should be to offset and stabilise such money demand shocks' (see Beckworth 2011a).

According to research published by the Federal Reserve Bank of St Louis, one reason money demand rose during 2014 was that low interest rates forced investors to switch from low-interest-bearing assets to assets that were more liquid (Wen and Arias 2014). But note that the Fed contributed to those low rates:

> In this regard, the unconventional monetary policy has reinforced the recession by stimulating the private sector's money demand through pursuing an excessively low interest rate policy.

This argument is not that the Federal Reserve causes low interest rates and a fall in velocity through their interest rates decisions. The Fed has limited market power, and its ability to 'control' interest rates is often overstated. Rather, there are multiple ways in which central banks can influence the demand for money. A crucial one is their communications.[17]

---

17 Consider, for example, Buiter (2009): 'Any central banker who argues, as some do, that "we set the overnight rate on reserves and we simply accommodate the demand for reserves at that (official policy) rate; therefore, until the official policy rate hits the zero floor there is no quantitative easing as a separate policy instrument" is delirious. This is because the demand for reserves depends not just on the official policy rate, but also other interest rates and spreads (on public and private assets of different maturities), some of which can be influenced by the central bank even when the official policy rate is kept constant. This is especially true during times when financial markets are illiquid and disorderly.'

Supplier-induced demand and central banks

The concept of supplier-induced demand (SID) rests on an information asymmetry. For example, in health economics we might believe that doctors (the agents) know more about a patient's medical condition than the patient does (the principals). In the case of central banking the information asymmetry could be in terms of an information advantage (i.e. access to privileged information),[18] or could just be as a result of discretionary monetary policy (hence the importance of 'Fed watching'). As Labelle et al. (1994) point out, we can think of SID in normative or positive terms. Normatively, we might be concerned that the principal will use their information advantage to encourage the patient to acquire more medical procedures than they actually need. We can view SID in this sense as circumventing market forces. Alternatively, we can take a positive view of SID whereby it leads to a shift in the patient's demand curve, 'to convince patients to increase their use of medical care without lowering the price charged' (Hadley et al. 1979: 247). Both approaches can work together, because we can make normative statements about the consequences of SID, without impugning bad motivations on any actors. Indeed Labelle et al. (1994: 352) make the case that the term 'induce' is appropriate:

> a) It does not specify self-interest as a motive for the 'inducer' and, b) it does not imply that inducement is

---

18 Central banks often talk up their information advantage, saying that 'if you've seen what we've seen you'd understand the need for dramatic policy'.

> necessarily bad for the 'inducee', or that it results in an
> action that necessarily runs contrary to his or her will
> ... indeed, one can make the argument that to 'induce' is
> exactly what the physician is supposed to be doing in his
> or her role as the patient's agent.

We can assume good intentions on the part of policy-makers. While some of the health literature may take it as given that doctors may seek to 'exploit' their information advantage for personal gain, the central bank does appear to believe it is acting in the public interest. Hence SID isn't a regrettable consequence of asymmetric information; it is part and parcel of the function of a central bank. We can define SID as the demand for money in excess of what would be present in a free banking regime. In other words, it is the additional demand for money generated by the central bank's actions, and which we can attribute to its status as a central bank. To be clear, the claim isn't that 'supply creates its own demand'; rather, the supplier has the potential to shift the demand curve.

It is well known in the health economics literature that certain tests are more likely to be carried out because the facilities exist, suggesting that it may be the existence of equipment that determines the demand for its use, as opposed to vice versa (see, for example, Consumer Reports 2012). In a central bank context, this ties into moral hazard in that things such as deposit insurance may be the result of a perceived demand, but once it exists it elicits a utilisation over and above what would otherwise be the case.

Factors that are generally assumed to increase SID are things such as direct marketing (Findlay 2001). There isn't a close parallel to this in terms of central banking, aside from the (not inconsequential) public education departments of central banks. The problem is in fact a lot deeper. According to White (2005), the entire character of academic research in monetary economics is shaped by the influence of the Federal Reserve. He points out the high ratios of Fed affiliations on the editorial boards of major journals, and the incentive to conduct research that would be valued by the Federal Reserve for any scholar interested in working for it.

In a 1994 survey Labelle et al. (1994) identified a lack of consensus among health economists as to the nature and importance of SID.[19] It is hard to simply 'apply' the SID to central banking because it is somewhat contested and ill defined. According to Labelle et al. (ibid.: 34), 'there are several different, and analytically distinct, types of supplier-induced demand … accordingly, there is no general agreement on the development and implementation of public policy based on the results'. Indeed even the emergence of subsequent conceptual frameworks is not really applicable to central banking. In the field of health economics, there is an opportunity for physicians

---

19 As an example of the lack of consensus in the SID literature (at the time), consider the fact that Labelle et al.'s (1994: 348) strongest evidence to claim that there was an emerging consensus is that 'Over eighty percent of respondents agreed with the statement "within broad limits, physicians generate demand for their services in response to economic incentives"'. To an economist, the fact that 20 per cent disagree is frightening!

to exploit their information advantage to persuade the patient to agree to unnecessary (or at least suboptimally high) treatment. In our case, the central bank isn't manipulating the agent's decision, but is actually causing (in part) the illness. Superficially, the central banker is the good guy. He is the firefighter seeking to protect the public. Whether he's abusing his information advantage to sell you more water than you actually need is of secondary importance. Ultimately, he's the reason you need liquidity in the first place. Perhaps people are less likely to consider the SID because it is so audacious – it's not a swindler that is masquerading as a firefighter but an arsonist!

To use an alternative analogy, imagine that there is a monopoly provider of flu vaccines. In that situation, if there is a flu pandemic that generates an increased demand for vaccinations, it would be wise for them to increase the quantity supplied as a result. However, they can hardly claim credit for fixing the problem if they themselves contributed to the scare. If government creates a panic about flu vaccine shortages, the solution isn't to supply more but to stop creating a panic.

When discussing the apparent failure of the Bank of Japan's use of 'non-standard' monetary policy to boost demand, William White (2012: 10) says:

> [P]erhaps the most important reason for this is that the demand for bank reserves tends to rise to match the increase in supply; in short, loan growth does not seem to be much affected.

'Target savers' are those who have a specific amount of savings in mind and interest rate cuts have the perverse effect of making them have to save an even greater share of their income. *The Economist* (2013a) explains how this ties in with uncertainty:

> Since negative real rates tend to occur at times of turmoil, people may simply become more cautious and save more. Government raids on bank deposits will only fuel their fears.

Indeed Frances Coppola (2013) argues that QE can be considered contractionary:

> The extra reserves provided by QE are in no sense expansionary. If anything, QE is contractionary, because it reduces the velocity of money in the financial system. When collateral is scarce, funding flows are impeded. There may be more actual funds available, but if they aren't moving, they aren't any use.

There is further evidence for this counterintuitive finding. According to *The Economist* (2014a) (which is summarising Prasad (2014)), 'the 2008 financial crisis might have been expected to erode the dollar's global prominence. Instead ... it cemented it. America's fragility was, paradoxically, a source of strength for its currency'. It is possible that emergency monetary policy *generates* the increase in the demand for money that it professes to be attempting to accommodate.

Regime uncertainty and big players[20]

The seminal account of regime uncertainty is Higgs (1997), which focuses on explaining the duration of the Great Depression. He argues that the main reason for the dramatic reduction in private sector investment from 1935 to 1940 was a specific type of uncertainty – namely, the uncertainty that investors felt about the security of their property rights and any related returns (ibid.: 563).[21] It is important to stress that the 'regime' being referred to is the private property rights regime, and that this applies from a tax rise that reduces the return on an asset to outright confiscation. As *The Economist* (2013d) says:

> What troubles businessfolk and investors most is the random nature of the process. They do not know where the next tax will be levied or regulatory boot descend. When rules are proposed, it can take ages for the details to emerge, making it hard for companies to plan ahead. That is the most insidious – and most underestimated – form of political risk.

Evans (2015) uses the criteria set out by Higgs (1997) to assess the extent to which regime uncertainty was prevalent

---

20 Parts of this section are reproduced from Evans (2013).

21 A longer definition is as follows: '[The] widespread inability to form confident expectations about future private property rights in all of their dimensions. Private property rights specify the property owner's rights to decide how property will be used, to accrue income from its uses, and to transfer these rights to others in various voluntary arrangements' (see Higgs 2011).

in 2008–11 in the UK.[22] Without attempting to quantify these factors, he found similarities. In the US during the Great Depression a change of regime from capitalism to some kind of economic nationalism was considered 'not only possible but likely' (Higgs 1997: 569). In the UK, although Andrew Lilico declares the 2008 bank nationalisations as being 'the end of private capitalism' (Lilico 2009a), it may be an exaggeration that downplays the extent of prevailing regulatory control, and neglects the intention of returning the banks to private hands after the crisis. Higgs's second indicator was punitive taxes on the wealthy, and he uses the 1935 Wealth Tax as evidence. It is telling that in April 2010 the Labour government raised the top rate of income tax (levied on incomes over £150,000) from 40 per cent to a symbolic 50 per cent. It is generally agreed that such a high rate reduces tax revenues, and so the rationale is political populism rather than economic necessity. In 2011 the Deputy Prime Minister vowed to 'get tough' on 'excessive boardroom pay' (BBC 2011), although this might be treated as rhetorical grandstanding rather than the genuine venom that Roosevelt seemed to possess.[23] The

---

22 A nice example of how it was prevalent in the US is the fact that it was Ben Bernanke himself who coined the term 'fiscal cliff' (*The Economist* 2012a).

23 Having said this, 'Project Marlin' was a negotiation exercise between government and major banks, and the aim was to alter compensation schemes so that they would be more in line with public sentiment. On 1 January 2011, Chancellor George Osborne surprised the industry by announcing a 7 per cent 'bank levy' on certain debts. This caused outrage because of the amounts and also the fact that it was unanticipated. It was originally aimed to draw in £2 billion of revenue but within a month had become a permanent policy that was seeking to raise £2.5 billion.

third factor that Higgs points to is constitutional changes that award more power to politicians. But 'the government was not seeking to bolster its economic policies with constitutional reform' (Evans 2015). Higgs uses rising membership of trade unions and their increased influence over the Democrats as his fourth factor. But in the UK these numbers were falling from 2009 to 2010. Higgs's fifth factor relates to the personality of the leader – in particular Roosevelt's 'hostility bordering on hatred for investors as a class' (Higgs 1997: 580). In all, while factors that contribute to regime uncertainty were present in the UK, they were on a significantly smaller scale. But this does not mean that it was not a relevant driver of economic events.

It is important to stress that regime uncertainty is an unintended consequence of policy interventions. There is a deep irony that policymakers make radical changes to try to restore economic stability, unaware that these changes are directly contributing to the instability. As *The Economist* (2013d) says, 'Arbitrary decisions by government may reduce business confidence, and thus inhibit the investment the politicians want to see.' Greenspan (2011: 165) claimed that 50–75 per cent of the fall in illiquid long-term investment was due to 'the shock of vastly greater uncertainties embedded in the competitive, regulatory and financial environments faced by business since the collapse of Lehman Brothers, deriving from the surge in government activism'. The communication policy of a central bank is a critical way to help market participants form expectations about future central bank actions. And, as *The Economist* (2013c) has argued, 'the crisis accelerated the reliance on communications as a means to stimulate the economy'.

According to Koppl (2002: 17), 'big players' are actors that combine three things. Firstly, they have the power to influence a market. Secondly, they have some sort of immunity from competition. And thirdly, they operate with discretion.[24] This provides a means to not only bolster the theory of regime uncertainty (by providing a channel through which expectations are formed), but demonstrates that the power of central banks extends beyond their ability to control interest rates. Even if Big Players aren't big enough to control a market, they can influence outcomes by introducing information that market participants need to respond to.

Despite not being able to observe uncertainty directly, there are different ways we can go about operationalising the concept. Rather than identify one in particular, it is helpful to consider an array.

Lars Christensen (2012) has advocated the subindex of 'Rule of Law' from the Economic Freedom Index as a measure of regime uncertainty. While capturing the concept outlined by Higgs very well, this is only really suited to providing broad trends and country-by-country comparisons. It is only released on an annual basis and is on a 20-point scale, meaning that it is fairly stable over

---

24 Elsewhere, Big Players have been defined as 'anyone who habitually exercises discretionary power to influence the market while himself remaining wholly or largely immune from the discipline of profit and loss' (Koppl and Yeager 1996: 368).

time. Unfortunately, it doesn't help us identify any causal influence that regime uncertainty may have in terms of recessions.

Other ways to empirically determine uncertainty (more broadly) rely on finding proxies. Evans (2012) splits these into two categories: volatility and chatter. Volatility has several direct measures. VIX is a measure of the volatility of the S&P 500 index, although concerns have been expressed about what it actually reveals.[25] The equivalent measure for the UK is the FTSE 100 Volatility Index. However, these fail to capture the inherent unpredictability of genuine (Knightian) uncertainty (see Knight 1921). They imply that uncertainty is high when the volatility is high. But this may just be a consequence of a rapid (and efficient) absorption of new information. Periods of apparent calm that are interspersed with step changes are more consistent with genuine uncertainty. Indeed you can buy futures contracts in volatility indices. The fact that we are aware of them, and pay attention to them, reveals that they fail to capture the type of uncertainty that concerns us.

Rather than measure volatility, an alternative approach is to look for signs that people are concerned about uncertainty. This could be from newspaper reports or business surveys, and they have been utilised as an important component of the 'Policy Uncertainty Index' created by Scott Baker, Nicholas Bloom and Steven Davis.[26] In addition to

---

25 For example, 'it seems that VIX is most closely correlated to absolute movements in the S&P 500, rather than changes in volatility' (Cookson 2014).

26 See http://policyuncertainty.com/index.html (accessed 11 July 2014).

news media references, they look at impending tax code expirations, and disagreement among forecasts with regard to inflation and government spending. It is a somewhat arbitrary mix, but reveals some important trends, as Figure 10 shows.

Figure 10 Policy uncertainty

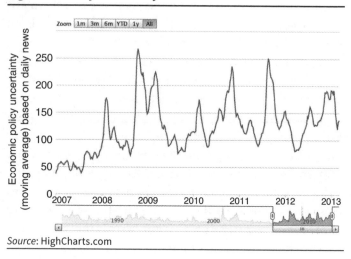

Source: HighCharts.com

The authors point to real options effects, financing costs and precautionary savings as the mechanisms by which uncertainty affects economic activity, but the components are selected to fit with a specific time period. The usefulness of the measure will only be evident once it has been applied to multiple periods of recession and recovery. But the compilation method is not necessarily suitable for comparisons over time: for example, the sources being used, and the particular terms searched may need to be updated. Leduc and Zheng (2012) use survey data to claim that policy uncertainty is a leading indicator over economic activity, resulting in a decline in aggregate demand, and Leduc and Zheng (2013: 4) find that it 'contributed significantly to the outward shift in the Beveridge curve during the economy recovery'.[27] Stein and Stone (2012) look at the implied volatility of almost 4,000 US firms by measuring the spread between the sale price of a share and the price at which it can be exercised. They find that around a third of the reduction in investment and job hires in 2008–10 were caused by elevated uncertainty. As *The Economist* (2013b) says, 'If the fiscal path were a little clearer, the reduction in uncertainty should spur investment and output, which in turn should improve the fiscal picture'.

Forward guidance also has the potential to increase uncertainty. In August 2013 the Bank of England made a commitment to keep interest rates at 0.5 per cent *at least* until unemployment fell below 7 per cent. Several 'knock-out' caveats were added that would give the MPC scope to abandon this pledge, namely: if the MPC forecast of inflation in 18–24 months' time rose above 2.5 per cent; if inflation expectations lost their anchor; or if the Financial Policy Committee (FPC) deemed the monetary stance to threaten financial stability. While this was intended to reduce uncertainty, it also introduced a new form of uncertainty into the system. Market participants had to

---

27 The Beveridge curve shows the relationship between vacancy and unemployment rates. Historically, it suggests a negative relationship between the two variables and outward shifts imply reductions in the efficiency of the labour market.

interpret how credible this commitment was, especially in light of disagreement over how quickly unemployment would fall and whether this would be a trigger for rate rises in and of itself. In its communication, the MPC wanted to emphasise the clear rule that binds their actions and therefore helps to shape expectations. However, it didn't reduce the amount of discretion involved in the decision about when to raise rates. Indeed in early 2014 real GDP growth for 2012 Q3 was significantly revised upwards (from 1.5 per cent, compared to the previous quarter, to 1.9 per cent). The Bank of England expected the 7 per cent unemployment threshold to be breached in 2016, but soon after launching forward guidance this seemed likely to occur as early as 2014.[28] Hence there was uncertainty about whether this would indeed provide a signal that the economy was strong enough to warrant an interest rate rise, or whether the MPC would simply move the goalposts. In February 2014 the MPC backtracked from the importance of the unemployment threshold, suggesting that this figure was only being used to tell markets that rates would stay low for longer than they were currently expecting. It was therefore not a policy rule that was being used to communicate how policy decisions would relate to trends in important indicators.

We need to be careful that we don't imply that any and all government action generates uncertainty, and thus,

---

28 It is hard to tell, but it seems more likely that this was as a result of new and unexpectedly positive economic data (that would have happened regardless), rather than changes in behaviour that were caused by forward guidance being adopted.

that policymakers should do nothing.[29] It is conceivable that, although some actions can make things worse, inaction is also a problem. Warren Buffett has said, 'if I didn't think the government was going to act, I would not be doing anything this week' (quoted in Paulson 2010: 284).

Just because we cannot measure uncertainty, it does not mean we cannot recognise it. It just means that our method should be a historical narrative. Before providing one, we need to be wary of two things. Firstly, although regime uncertainty is a powerful tool to see how changes in expectations affect the economy, and how policy intervention can have negative unintended consequences, it is telling that the milder 'policy' uncertainty has generated greater empirical attention. One challenge is to understand whether we view regime uncertainty as simply an extreme form of policy uncertainty (i.e. once policy uncertainty reaches a certain level it starts to challenge the regime). Also, these studies tend to take place in capitalist societies while they are in a financial crisis. Hence they tend to show reductions in the quality of policy. If we think about tax reform, few people are happy with taxes in their present state. So stability is rarely seen as a quality in and of itself. The issue is predictability. Presumably the same thing applies to policy more generally – but even if predictability is more important than stability, the direction matters. If the status quo is inhospitable then regime

---

29 This also raises an issue about whether uncertainty implies that investors hold off on investment (this is argued by Bernanke 1983), or alters the *types* of investment they make (such as moving into gold, as argued by Higgs 1997).

or policy uncertainty would be a precursor to successful outcomes. Hence we need to disentangle whether it is uncertainty that is the problem, or the bad policies that are being adopted.

The second danger in the search for regime uncertainty is that we have to be aware of false positives. Instead of looking for examples of bad outcomes that can be attributed to political uncertainty, we should also study events that one might expect to lead to uncertainty, but do not. For example, in 2010 the UK general election resulted in a Conservative–Liberal Democrat coalition. One might argue that this was broadly in line with the expectation that there would be no clear winner, and hence already priced in. But few people anticipated a coalition being formed, let alone lasting for the full term. The fact that markets barely budged is surprising. A second example is the appointment of Mark Carney as Governor of the Bank of England. When the BBC listed five front-runners for the job, he wasn't even on the list. Following a personal request from the Chancellor, and an agreement to reduce the term, his surprise appointment was announced on 26 November 2012. His reputation was for relatively radical monetary policy tools (such as forward guidance) and alternative policy targets (such as NGDP). Even though the Governor is just one vote among nine on the MPC, his ability to frame that debate makes him clearly a 'Big Player'. Indeed even if he were unable to command a majority vote it would seem reasonable to assume that if he favoured a change in the monetary policy framework this would have been discussed with the Chancellor before the appointment. And yet, once again markets barely moved. If these two events don't generate uncertainty, it demonstrates the difficulty in attempting to measure (and indeed understand) its impact on the economy.

On 14 September 2007 Northern Rock Bank sought emergency liquidity provisions from the UK government. While Paulson and Bernanke would be giving daily updates to the press and actually stoking uncertainty by exaggerating the problems facing the economy,[30] the Chancellor and Governor of the Bank of England didn't even meet in person, and waited for three days before they made a public statement (see Walters 2008: 64). The reason for this inactivity seems to be Mervyn King's commitment to a Bagehot-esque concern for moral hazard, wanting to penalise banks for seeking emergency support (see Brummer 2009: 66). His instinct was to launch a covert rescue but this was impossible under the 2005 Market Abuses Act (see Evans 2015). Hence he dithered. He was also unsure whether there would be an increase in deposit insurance and therefore refrained from making a public commitment to reassure depositors. Consequently, the BBC reported that Northern Rock was in severe financial difficulty, and the explanation of the insufficient scale of deposit insurance

---

30 According to Paulson, 'I knew I had to choose my words carefully. We faced a real dilemma: to get Congress to act we needed to make dire predictions about what would happen to the economy if we didn't get the authorities we wanted. But doing so could backfire. Frightened consumers might stop spending and start saving, which was the last thing we needed right then. Investors could lose the final shred of the confidence that was keeping the markets from crashing' (Paulson 2010: 281–82). Indeed he'd warned Chris Dodd 'all we'll do is spook the markets' (ibid.: 150).

created panic. This prompted a bank run (see Peston 2008: 178). The Bank of England didn't start to cut interest rates (their main policy signal) until December 2007, and only then by 0.25 per cent. So although uncertainty can be hard to measure, it is highly important.

In terms of attempts to measure regime uncertainty, Higgs's (1997) primary focus was on private sector investment. Figure 11 shows private investment growth in the UK from 2007 to 2016.[31]

Figure 11 Private investment, 2007–16 (year-on-year % growth)

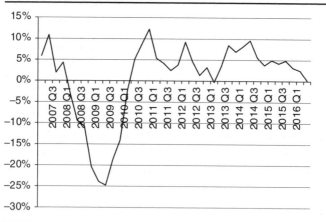

In 2008 Q1 private investment was £65.4 billion, but it fell dramatically to £47.65 billion by 2009 Q2. Indeed this trough constituted a –24 per cent growth rate and coincides with the negative velocity shock shown earlier. A

---

31 'Private investment' is the sum of business investment and private sector investment, and is published by Kaleidic Economics: http://www.kaleidic. org/data (accessed 26 August 2016).

collapse of this sort of magnitude is what regime uncertainty is intended to help explain.

Conclusion

In this chapter I have tried to make a simple claim. Part of the increase in the demand for central bank reserves is a result of the information asymmetry between a discretionary central bank and the general public. If aggregate demand falls, then it must either be as a result of a reduction in the money supply or a reduction in velocity. It is common to think of the role of the central bank as to offset exogenous shocks to velocity, and indeed central bankers may point to the inherent difficulties of doing so to explain why they sometimes fail. However, the money supply is not the sole weapon of the monetary authorities. They also influence the demand for money and their actions can be an underlying cause of velocity shocks. Thus policies such as QE aren't merely a central bank's response to external events; they are also shaping those events. White (2010) and Hummel (2011) provide convincing arguments that during the financial crisis the Federal Reserve went beyond its traditional role as monetary authority to violate the rule of law and become a bona fide central planner of credit. The rise in the demand for money (and fall in velocity) that contributed to the 2008 collapse in nominal spending was not an additional event that the central bank had to contend with. It was a response to increased uncertainty that the central bank itself propagated. Velocity shocks are a consequence of monetary incompetence.

4 P: THE HIDDEN INFLATION OF THE GREAT MODERATION

Summary of key points

- Level targets have a stronger economic rationale than growth targets (such as inflation) but the Bank of England currently operates more of a hybrid.
- The Bank of England fan charts are flawed and less attention should be paid to them. Index-linked contracts are an imperfect way to protect against inflation because inflation entails relative price changes, as well as a fall in purchasing power.
- From 1999 to 2006, the Consumer Prices Index (CPI) systematically underreported the inflationary pressure in the UK. A rudimentary impact summary estimates the effect to be approximately 5.87 percentage points. More attention should be given to indices that include asset prices.
- While inflation is always and everywhere a monetary phenomenon, it is not necessarily always a consumer price one.

I shall try to show that (a) the price level is frequently a misleading guide to monetary policy and that its stability is no sufficient safeguard against crises and depressions, because (b) a credit expansion has a much deeper and more fundamental influence on the whole economy, especially on the structure of production, than that expressed in the mere change of the price level. The principal defect of those theories is that they do not distinguish between a fall of prices which is due to an actual contraction of the circulating medium and a fall in prices which is caused by a lowering of cost as a consequence of inventions and technological improvements.

Haberler (1996: 46–47)

Introduction

According to conventional wisdom, inflation was low in the years leading up to the financial crisis. However, this chapter argues that there was more inflationary pressure than is commonly accepted, and tries to reveal some of it. Indeed, the problem wasn't merely a faulty inflation indicator, but also the fact that inflation was being targeted in the first place. The UK adopted inflation targeting in October 1992 and it coincided with a lengthy period of low and stable inflation, low interest rates and stable GDP growth. In May 1997 the incoming Labour government decided to make the Bank of England independent, and from June 2008 the Monetary Policy Committee (MPC) was given authority to make monetary policy decisions. Its independence was only operational, however, since they were given the task of hitting an inflation target and limitations over the tools at their disposal.

This period of relative calm was a global phenomenon and has since become known as the Great Moderation.[1] Nunes and Cole (2013) provide a list of possible reasons for the Great Moderation: favourable changes in the structure of the economy; beneficial technology shocks; lack of negative shocks; better monetary policy; a mirage. There is no doubt that each of these factors played a role. The focus of this chapter is to consider the extent to which the Great Moderation was in fact an illusion, one that was masked by faulty inflation data and a flawed inflation-targeting regime.

It is conventional to look at price indices for evidence of loose monetary policy. When talking about Japan, for example, John Greenwood says, 'the puzzle about this period is not so much the scale of the asset price inflation, but the relative lack of inflation at the CPI level' (Greenwood 2006: 144). But this shouldn't always be taken as a given. As William White has remarked, 'another awkward fact revealed by historical studies is that many deep slumps have not been preceded by high inflation' (White 2010). He points to the US in the 1920s, Japan in the 1990s and South East Asia in 1997/98 as examples. Helpfully, a key aspect of the Austrian theory of the business cycle is the fact that consumer prices are a flawed way to judge whether there is an unsustainable boom taking place. According to Roger Garrison, 'the market process set in motion by credit expansion does not depend in any essential way on there being a change in the general level of prices' (Garrison 2001: 71). He uses the

---

1   Wallison (2011) dates it from 1982 to 2007.

example of the 1920s to explain how the upward pressure from credit growth can be offset by downward pressure from output growth.

In the build-up to the financial crisis and subsequent recession there was a common opinion that the inflationary environment was benign. Those who used money supply data to forewarn of bubble activity were met with a simple question: why is CPI on target? Instead of generating the Great Moderation, this chapter will argue that inflation targeting simultaneously concealed an inflationary boom (because CPI is a faulty indicator) and also partly caused the boom (because inflation targeting is a perverse policy tool).

The first section contrasts inflation targeting with price-level targets and argues that inflation targeting prompts counterintuitive policy decisions. The second section challenges the quality of CPI forecasts by looking at the Bank of England's fan charts. And the third section provides a critique of the CPI as a measure of inflation (and indicator of the monetary stance) by presenting six issues: a compilation error relating to sales; the timing of the change of target; the formula effect; neglecting early stage inflation; neglecting housing prices; and neglecting asset prices more generally. The final section looks at a seventh criticism of CPI, arguing that productivity improvements conceal actual price inflation. It provides calculations of a 'productivity norm' to reveal where the price level and CPI growth rates might have been had productivity changes been allowed to manifest themselves as lower prices.

Inflation vs price-level targets

Lilico (2009b) argues that a price-level target (i.e. a commitment to keep inflation growing along a specified target path) is preferable to an inflation target (a commitment to keep inflation at a specified annual rate). He lists four downsides to inflation targets. Firstly, the long-term price level (and therefore inflation rate) is less certain under inflation targeting, because bygones are not bygones. If an unexpected shock takes the price level away from its designated path, an inflation target will simply ensure that it returns to its specified growth rate from then onwards. A price-level target, by contrast, will allow the inflation rate to change such that the price level returns to the previous path. Figure 12 shows the difference.

Figure 12 Inflation and price level (under inflation expectations)

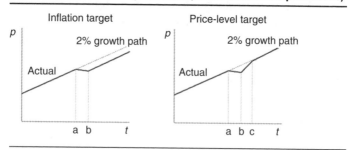

In the case of an inflation target, we can see that a single negative shock causes the actual price level to deviate from the 2 per cent growth path. If there are multiple shocks it becomes incredibly difficult to predict where the price level will be in the medium term. By contrast, the price-level target shows that if a negative shock occurs (at time period a), the monetary authority will then be obliged to offset it, and generate sufficient inflation to return to trend (points b to c). In short, a level target brings the indicator back in line with expectations. A growth target constantly resets. Hence, level targets generate more long-term stability.

A second downside with inflation targets is that short-term inflation may be more volatile than level targets (and any volatility they do have will be more uncertain). Lilico argues that inflation rate targets attempt to alter the inflation rate in proportion to the *size* of any output gap, while price-level targets will alter it in proportion to *changes* in the output gap. As he says (ibid.: 12):

> [I]f there are moderate nominal rigidities (so that output shocks are moderately persistent) and significant output shocks are sufficiently rare (so that the unwinding of output shocks is, on average, the main driver of changes in output) then the volatility of the short-term inflation rate will be lower under price-level targeting than under inflation targeting.

The third issue with inflation targets is that uncertainty over future inflation adds risk premia to interest rates, and thus reduces growth rates. This occurs because index-linked contracts are an imperfect way to protect against inflation risk. Moreover, while index-linked contracts can protect against a fall in purchasing power, as measured against a specific index, they cannot protect

against the relative price changes that inflation necessarily generates.[2] And fourthly, Lilico argues that inflation targeting requires more fine-tuning. This is because
under inflation targeting there is an inflationary bias due
to the temptation to generate surprise inflation, and also
because a price-level target can be maintained by market
forces (provided it is credible). Svensson (1999) also finds
that price-level targeting reduces long-term price variability, eliminates an inflation bias, and may in fact have less
short-run inflation variability than inflation targeting. The
bottom line here is that an attempt to generate short-term
stability (with an inflation target) has a tendency to create
long-term uncertainty. By contrast, a willingness to tol-
erate short-term volatility (under a price-level target) will
lead to long-term stability.

Lilico (2009b) also points out two issues relating to
the Great Moderation that give further reasons for why
level targets are better than growth targets. One is the
fact that inflation targets tend to be asymmetric. As he
points out, 'during the 1990s and 2000s, inflation was not
happily permitted to go below target to accommodate
the small China or internet cost-reducing effects each
year, but the oil price spike of 2008 was accommodated'
(ibid.: 14).

---

2   US investors can protect themselves against 'inflation' by buying Treasury
    Inflation Protected Services (TIPS). Shelton (2012) proposes the adoption
    of Treasury Trust Bonds (TTBs), which offer the owners a choice between a
    nominal dollar return or a pre-specified quantity of gold. Having an array
    of these types of instrument would provide important clues as to whether
    inflationary risk is being fully captured by CPI protection.

He also links inflation targeting to asset cycles. When liquidity is injected into an economy that the monetary authority fears may slip below target inflation, 'if the regime is credible that extra money won't go into current expenditure but instead goes into financial assets to save against the day that the inflation targeter will hike interest rates aggressively to mop up the liquidity' (ibid.: 15). Crucially, 'because the money is in financial assets, it isn't turning into measured inflation (immediately), so the inflation targeter doesn't need to mop up the liquidity early, even if the money drives up asset prices' (ibid.: 15).[3]

According to Dittmar et al. (1999: 33; see also Dittmar and Gavin 2000):

> For policymakers who believe that the central bank can, and should, stabilize the business cycle, it is a drawback of inflation-targeting regimes that in order to reduce inflation uncertainty, the central bank must ignore the state of the real economy. We show how this drawback may be overcome by putting just a small weight on a long-term price level objective.

But if these arguments suggest that price-level targets may be preferable to inflation targets, why are inflation targets more common? One reason is precisely because they have a shorter time horizon – this makes policymakers more accountable: 'an inflation target offers politicians the

---

3   Lilico also makes the case that a price-level target makes it less likely that you get caught in a liquidity trap type situation (Lilico 2009b: 116).

opportunity to be judged on something concrete over a reasonable political timescale' (Lilico 2009b: 18). According to Coletti et al. (2008), the benefits of switching from an inflation targeting to a price-level targeting regime are relatively modest. And Kryvtsov et al. (2008) point out that there would be switching costs, especially if the need to generate credibility necessitated a recession.

Lilico argues that 'average-inflation targeting' is a sort of inflation target/price-level target hybrid. He says, 'an incoming government would state its target (say 2.0%) for the average inflation rate over the next Parliament' (Lilico 2009b: 18). It should be clear that as the time horizon of an average-inflation target regime lengthens it approaches a price-level target. Perhaps this is what we currently have. The Bank of England holds a competition called 'Target Two Point Zero' where it invites UK schools to simulate being on the MPC. In the instruction pack it claims that 'The aim is to set the degree of policy stimulus that we think gives the best chance of inflation being 2.0% in around two years' time'. It also says that 'Monetary policy is aiming to ensure that the inflation rate is 2.0% on average over time' (Bank of England 2013: 32).

Notice that the former is worded like a forward-looking inflation target, while the latter sounds more like a level target. If inflation were 4 per cent for each of the previous two years, and 2 per cent this year, then the former would imply that policy should be unchanged (all else equal). However, the latter implies it should be below 2 per cent. In any case, it is curious that the Bank of England displays the current inflation rate in the 'Key Facts' section of its website, rather than inflation expectations two years hence.[4]

Fan charts

In 1993 the Bank of England began to publish a chart showing its 'central projection' of inflation over the subsequent two years, together with a band of uncertainty. In February 1996 this was updated with a chart that captured an entire probability density function, with lighter shading to represent wider confidence intervals (see Dowd 2004). They tend to look eight quarters ahead and are called 'fan charts' because over time the range within which inflation is likely to fall becomes wider and wider.

In August 1997 the Bank started to make available the underlying calculations upon which its projections are based. The fan charts are an important tool of monetary policy. They help to set inflation expectations and shed a light on the decision-making process of the MPC. There have been several attempts to test their reliability. Dowd (2004: 108) found that 'the model over-estimates inflation risk at all horizons' and that there was a tendency for this over-estimation to 'increase with the length of the horizon'. Wallis (2003: 165) finds that although the current-quarter forecasts are reasonably well calibrated, for the one-year ahead forecasts, 'The fan charts fan out too quickly and the excessive concern with the upside

---

4   See http://www.bankofengland.co.uk/Pages/home.aspx (accessed 27 March 2015).

risks was not justified over the period considered'. Wallis (2004: 71) incorporates subsequent data and finds that they 'overstated forecast uncertainty'. Dowd (2008: 86) assesses the inflation fan charts published by the Swedish Riksbank and finds 'evidence that forecasts deteriorate as the horizon increases'.[5] If fan charts from different countries exhibit similar biases, this may suggest a problem with the underlying method.

Dowd (2007a) used the Bank's own model and parameter forecasts to conclude that there was only a 1.9 per cent chance of not breaching the target range of 1.5–3.5 per cent from 1997 Q4 to 2004 Q1. He points out that there are two ways to interpret this: either the Bank was very lucky that CPI happened to stay within these limits or, alternatively, the model overstates inflation volatility. He highlights a tension between the model, 'which seems to suggest a significant risk of inflation breaching this range', and how inflation actually behaved, 'which, *ex post*, looks as though there was never any serious danger of the breach occurring' (ibid.: 93). As he says (ibid.: 99):

> What needs to be explained is the co-existence of two apparently incongruent phenomena – the high degree of inflation uncertainty shown by the MPC's fan chart forecasts, on the one hand, and the low and stable inflation

5   Having said this, we should not really treat the fan charts as being 'forecasts' per se. As Cronin and Dowd (2013: 12) point out, 'all fan chart projections are a species of scenario analysis: they do not give forecast per se, but only stochastic projection of what *might* happen *if* certain scenarios unfold'.

actually delivered by the MPC's own monetary policy, on the other.

According to Dowd, 'one is tempted to suggest that the main problem with the fan charts is, quite simply, the fact that they fan out'. Indeed even a cursory glance at one shows a remarkable discontinuity. Dowd's study was published in 2007, so let's consider the fan chart from the August 2006 Inflation Report, shown in Figure 13 (on the next page).

The range of the fan chart encourages the view that while inflation is expected to return to target, it could plausibly go quite far outside the range of historic inflation. In the previous five years, inflation stayed within a band of 1.0–2.4 per cent, and yet the fan chart implies that over the next two years there's a more than 10 per cent chance of it being outside a 1–3 per cent range. According to Dowd (2007b: 18), the historic behaviour of inflation 'suggests a mean-reverting process whereas the fan chart forecasts suggest some kind of diffusion process'. Dittmar et al. (1999: 25) argue that 'a period-by-period inflation-targeting regime causes the error in forecasts of the price-level to rise with the forecast horizon', but this shouldn't apply to a forecast of the inflation *rate*. Indeed the fact that it fans out at all is a fairly worrying thing since it implies that as time passes the Bank of England is more likely to lose control of future inflation than close in on the target. Surely – if the central bank is credibly committed to an inflation target – temporary/surprise deviations from target should be considered more likely that those occurring four years hence.

Figure 13 August 2006 fan chart

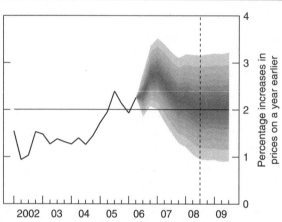

Source: Bank of England Inflation Report, August 2006 (https://www.bankof
england.co.uk/-/media/boe/files/inflation-report/2006/august-2006.pdf,
page 8).

Interestingly (especially in light of the previous section on inflation targeting versus price-level targeting), Dowd points out that one explanation for the odd finding is that the model probably assumes a pure inflation target. If there is a hybrid regime (such as an inflation averaging one discussed earlier, or a part inflation target part price-level target), then (Dowd 2007a: 100)

> if the central bank ... places even a small weight on the past price level path, then the inflation rate will be considerably more stable than it would have been had the central bank followed a 'pure' inflation target alone and let past inflation bygones be bygones.

Figure 14 August 2008 fan chart

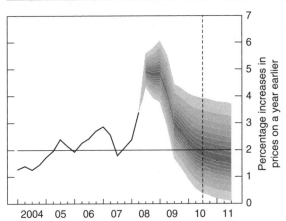

Source: Bank of England Inflation Report, August 2008 (https://www.
bankofengland.co.uk/-/media/boe/files/inflation-report/2008/august-2008.
pdf, page 8).

In fact, Dowd's work was published just before the fan charts failed spectacularly and the Bank's forecasts were shown to be hopelessly conservative. The actual inflation rate in September 2008 (i.e. two years after the publication of the chart) was 5.2 per cent. It's worth emphasising that the Bank assigns a 90 per cent probability value of inflation falling within the shaded range. Not only was actual inflation outside of this range, it was literally off the chart!

Figure 14 shows the August 2008 inflation chart (notice the change in the Y-axis compared with Figure 13).

The problem is that the Bank of England developed a reputation for over-estimating the threat of missing the inflation target. The experience of 2002–6 was that hitting the inflation target was even easier than the Bank expected. In fact, it proved to be significantly harder.

Price indices

The costs of looking at the wrong price index are severe. One of the biggest policy mistakes of the twentieth century was when Britain returned to the gold standard at the pre-war parity. Keynes's explanation for why this happened was that Churchill was 'gravely misled by his experts' (Keynes 1963: 249), who used a wholesale price index to make a comparison with America. Such an index largely comprises widely tradable raw materials, which are relatively flexible. As Alchian and Klein (1973: 185) point out, this 'significantly underestimated the extent of the necessary deflation' – the money wages of dockers in Liverpool are a lot stickier, for example. An obvious way to mitigate some of the costs of inflation is to use index-linked contracts. However, these don't fully solve the problem. A reason for the rarity of index-linked contracts is that any individual price index is an imperfect measure of what any individual person wants to protect themselves from. Indeed, 'the fact people don't use price indices for long term contracts more, suggests concerns about such indices being good measures of what actually happens to "the price level"' (ibid.).

The two traditional methods of measuring the price of baskets of goods over time are a Laspeyres index and a Paasche index. The former uses the initial quantities and thus tends to be biased upwards since consumers would be expected to switch to lower-priced goods. By contrast, a Paasche index utilises subsequent quantities, but as a result tends to take longer to compile. As Selgin (1988) points out, there are three issues that need to be addressed when constructing a price index: the choice of goods and services to include in the basket, the measure of central tendency (this is necessary in order to summarise the basket in a single figure) and the weights assigned to each item. These are the 'practical difficulties that frustrate construction of a reliable price index' (ibid.: 97).

All of these choices are somewhat arbitrary and all of them likely to change over time. Arthur Marget (1942: 33) used the term 'swarm' to capture the way in which prices change in an economy, and argued that unless most prices were changing by the average amount, an index would be misleading (see Egger 1995: 15). This addresses an important difference between how monetarists and Austrian school economists approach inflation. Whereas the former are concerned more about an index displaying a large average, the latter are more worried about the variance (of the individual prices).

It is well known that policymakers can tamper with official statistics. The term 'suppressed inflation' refers to the practice of masking a fall in the value of money by altering the method by which inflation measures are compiled (McCulloch 1975: 36–39). This isn't the claim being made here, however. And the points that follow are not criticisms of price indices per se. They are a combination of several different problems that specifically affected the CPI in the years leading up to the financial crisis. Taken together, they are evidence that policymakers – to the extent that they were using CPI as their measure of inflation – may have been ignoring inflationary pressure.[6]

Compilation error

The first issue relates to the way in which CPI measured sales. The Bank of England's February 2011 Inflation Report revealed an important error in previous CPI figures. In a seemingly innocuous text box it admitted, 'Previous collection methods may have biased down estimates of CPI clothing prices', because prices were only surveyed during winter and summer sales.[7] They estimated that had they been measured correctly (i.e. including prices from throughout the year), aggregate annual CPI from 1997 to 2009 would have been 0.3 percentage points higher. It is hard to say whether this would have been sufficient to elicit a change in policy, but it would have meant that CPI would have first gone above target in 2005 Q1 (rather than 2005 Q2), and would have necessitated a letter to the Chancellor (for breaching a 3 per cent limit) in 2006 Q4 (rather than 2008 Q2). The CPI warning light should have flashed, but it hadn't been correctly measured.

---

6   Sanderson et al. (2014) found that the Laspeyres index provided a lower inflation measure than the official CPI but these differences were small and unfortunately only covered 2008–9.

7   Inflation Report, February 2011, Bank of England.

The timing of the change of target

In 2003 the Bank of England switched its inflation target from RPIX to the CPI.[8] The main reason for this was harmonisation with other EU countries. However, it masked existing inflation in two important ways. Firstly, at the time of the switch RPIX was running at 2.9 per cent, which was 40 basis points above the target rate of 2.5 per cent. But CPI was 1.4 per cent, which was 60 basis points *below* the new target of 2 per cent. As Figure 15 (on the next page) shows, RPIX was below target for the bulk of its use, and CPI was under target on its introduction.

Under the previous regime there was pressure to tighten monetary policy, but for totally non-economic reasons monetary policy suddenly appeared to be too tight. In the words of then-member of the MPC, Stephen Nickell, this switch 'will involve slightly looser monetary policy for a limited period than would otherwise be the case' (see Thomas 2009: 7).

Indeed in the year before the switch the average growth rate of RPIX was 2.81 (i.e. 0.31 percentage points above target), while in the year following the switch the average growth rate of CPI was 1.32 (0.68 percentage points below target). The second reason why this shift in emphasis concealed inflation is that, although RPIX excludes mortgage

---

8   The reason the Bank targeted RPIX rather than RPI is that variable rate mortgages are closely linked to the Bank rate of interest. This creates a perverse situation because if inflation were too high and caused the Bank to raise interest rates, this would increase mortgage costs and hence increase RPI.

interest repayments, it does contain housing costs. The political decision to become aligned with other countries resulted in inflationary warning signs from housing costs being treated as a matter of financial stability, rather than monetary policy.

Figure 15 RPIX and CPI, 1997–2009[9]

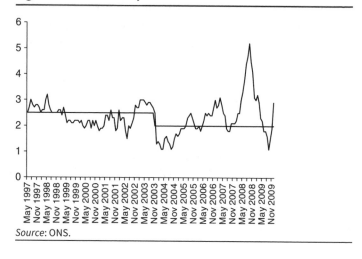

Source: ONS.

The formula effect

CPI and RPI not only measure different items, but they also use different formulae. In 2012 the ONS began a consultation to calculate RPI (which uses arithmetic averaging) in the same way as CPI (which uses geometric). At the time, this 'formula effect' boosted RPI by 0.88 percentage points

---

9   May 1997 to November 2003 and December 2003 to December 2009 respectively, monthly growth rate, with target rates.

overall (Aldrick 2012), and for the category of clothing and footwear it meant that while CPI was growing at 3.6 per cent, RPI was 12.6 per cent (Giles 2011).

Once again, statisticians are being constrained by politicians rather than economists because legislation constrains their ability to make changes.[10] But since there are infinite ways to construct a price index, a key decision is whether the measure should follow theoretical soundness, or whatever delivers a particular result. It is telling that the debate about the formula effect is in terms of how to bring RPI into line with CPI. The alternative view would be that CPI is underreporting inflation and should be brought into line with RPI.

Neglecting early-stage inflation

An even bigger source of the hidden inflation is revealed within an alternative inflation index. The Producer Price Index (PPI) measures the changes in prices paid for and received by domestic manufacturers. Although manufacturing is steadily falling as a share of the UK economy, in absolute terms it is still important. PPI can be split into

---

10 As already discussed, sometimes this legislation is intended to ensure compatibility with other countries. For countries that have the same currency it is obviously important to measure inflation the same way, which is why the EU adopted the Harmonised Index of Consumer Prices (HICP). It is also important to constrain the ability of politicians to make expedient changes. For example, in June 2010 the UK government began linking benefit payments to CPI rather than RPI. Given that CPI was lower than RPI, this saved around £4 billon a year (Aldrick 2012). It would obviously be concerning if the compilation methods were subject to change and influenced by policymakers.

input prices (i.e. raw materials) and output prices (or 'factory gate'). Figure 16 shows a comparison between the CPI and the input PPI.[11]

Figure 16 CPI and PPI, May 1997–Dec 2009 (monthly data, % change from previous year).

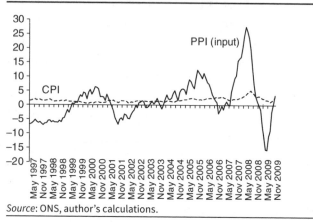

Source: ONS, author's calculations.

Firstly, prices for capital goods are more volatile than for consumer goods. Secondly, after a deflationary period that coincided with the technology crash, PPI started to outpace CPI, reaching almost 27.6 per cent at the onset of the recession. From May 2004 to November 2006 PPI was above 2 per cent (with the exception of December 2004), reaching 12.4 per cent in December 2005.

Focusing on the producer – as opposed to the consumer – side of the economy also reveals something interesting

---

11 The Office for National Statistics does not release PPI growth rates in a series. These estimates are based on an approximation of those growth rates using the levels (base year = 2010).

about the period of the Great Moderation. As Table 3 shows, the CPI and PPI measures are fairly similar from 1997 to 2009. However, if we look at Q1 2002 – Q4 2007 we can see clear evidence of hidden inflation.

Table 3   CPI vs PPI (input)

	CPI	PPI (input)
May 1997 – Dec 2009	Mean: 1.78% Median: 1.60%	Mean: 1.67% Median: 1.10%
Jan 2003 – Dec 2007	Mean: 1.88% Median: 1.90%	Mean: 3.81% Median: 3.05%

Neglecting housing prices

For those warning of asset bubbles in the build-up to the financial crisis, the obvious evidence was occurring in the housing market. However, it was not until March 2013 that the ONS introduced a measure of CPI that includes a measure of owner occupiers' housing costs (OOH), called CPIH (see Restieaux 2013). Unfortunately, this is only available from Jan 2005 to Dec 2012, but it reveals that CPIH was constantly higher than CPI. In the period Jan 2006 to Jul 2008 the average difference was 0.09 percentage points.

Neglecting asset prices more generally

Perhaps the most obvious place to look for hidden inflation is asset prices. Alchian and Klein (1973) provide the seminal account of why 'a price index used to measure inflation must include asset prices' (ibid.: 173). They argue that in order to capture all of the costs that enter someone's utility function, the spot prices of current consumption goods are not sufficient. You also need the current cash price of future consumption services (ibid.: 176).[12] Their proposal to replace CPI with a measure of 'current consumer services flow price inflation' is theoretically sound. As they say, 'our price index answers the standard textbook question of whether an individual needs more or less money to remain at the same level of satisfaction' (ibid.: 186).

The downside is that it is a lot harder to determine empirically. But we can use theory to acknowledge that it provides a further source of hidden inflation. Alchian and Klein use the example of the 1969–70 reduction in the growth rate of narrow money. They point out that CPI actually increased (from 5.8 per cent in late 1969 to 6.0 per cent in early 1970), giving the impression that money wasn't tightening. And yet stock indices fell dramatically (some by 30 per cent) and real interest rates rose. They claim that 'this evidence suggests that asset prices declined relative to flow prices over the period and that movements in the CPI severely underestimate the deflationary effects of the tight money policy' (ibid.: 181). Similarly, while the mean CPI for the UK from 2003 to 2007 was 1.89 per cent, the FTSE 100 rose by over 40 per cent.[13] Hence we can make the reverse claim to the one made by Alchian and Klein

---

12 They say that the index 'must include all assets – consumer and producer, durable and nondurable, tangible and intangible, financial and nonfinancial, human and nonhuman. All sources of present and future consumption services much be considered' (Alchian and Klein 1973: 177).

13 https://uk.finance.yahoo.com/echarts?s=%5EFTSE#symbol=%5EFTSE; range=1d

– CPI severely underestimated the inflation effects of loose money policy.[14]

Goodhart (2001: F335) claims that Alchian and Klein's argument has 'never, in my view, been successfully refuted on a *theoretical* plane' and this provides additional weight behind the idea that 'an analytically correct measure of inflation should take account of asset price changes'. He argues that while introducing volatility into the measure, 'some asset prices, notably housing, are closely associated with the main trend in inflation, and via "bubbles and busts" with output disturbances' (ibid.).[15] For the UK context, a former member of the Bank of England's MPC, Posen (2011) provides an overview of why policymakers should respond to asset prices. Consequently, economists who are serious about business cycles should want inflation measures that draw upon the asset classes where asset inflation is likely to turn up.

Productivity norm

The six issues presented in the previous section all suggest that there was more inflationary pressure in the UK in 1999–2006 than was being revealed in the CPI. A further place to look for 'hidden' inflation lies in understanding the impact of productivity on the general price level. All else equal, if

---

14 Going further, we can say that this effect will be bigger the stronger the interest rate channel is (Friedman and Schwartz 1963a; see Alchian and Klein 1973: 179).

15 Although a broader inflation measure that draws upon assets is indeed likely to increase volatility, it could be considered more robust to errors such as the one that underestimated CPI by 0.3 per cent for over a decade!

productivity is high (i.e. we can produce more with less) we might expect consumer prices to *fall*. If they do not (for example, as a consequence of a fixed inflation target), then contained CPI could be misleading. In terms of the dynamic equation of exchange, we can say the following:

$$M + V = P + Y.$$

The Y variable is a measure of real output growth, and this will tend to be driven by real productivity. In a real business cycle model Y is not only derived from the Solow growth rate, but *is* the Solow growth rate. The economy is deemed to always be growing at potential. The implication of this is that any increase in aggregate demand ($M + V$) will manifest itself in inflation (P) alone. However, if money is non-neutral, it will take time for such prices to adjust. New Keynesians and Austrians alike would posit that while prices adjust aggregate demand shocks influence not only prices, but also real growth. This adjustment process would allow output to deviate from potential.[16] In other words, a productivity norm would mean that positive productivity shocks (which would raise Y) will result in falling prices (see Horwitz 2000: 99):

$$M + V = P\downarrow + Y\uparrow.$$

However, an inflation target (or price-level stability) implies the following:

---

16 Evans (2016b) provides a graphical exposition of these shocks and clarifies the distinction between real output growth (Y) and the potential growth rate (Y^*). In equilibrium, $Y = Y^*$, however, while prices adjust we need a short-run aggregate supply curve to show that Y can deviate from Y^*.

$$M\!\uparrow + V = \bar{P} + Y\!\uparrow.$$

This increase in M will constitute a loosening of monetary policy that may not immediately show up in the CPI. In a monetary regime that is committed to 2 per cent inflation, two major outcomes occur. Firstly, consumers miss out on cheaper prices for goods and services (the true gains from innovation), as their wage growth lags behind inflation. Secondly, increases in the money supply will not necessarily reach consumer prices since they are masked by productivity gains. While many policymakers may assume that falling prices will delay purchases and stunt growth, Friedman and Schwartz (1963b: 15) have shown that during the nineteenth century the price level fell significantly and yet 'economic growth proceeded at a rapid rate'.

The 'productivity norm' was pioneered by Selgin (1997: 10) and is based on the theoretical assertion that:

> [T]he price level should be allowed to vary to reflect changes in goods' unit costs of production ... permanent improvements in productivity would be allowed to lower prices permanently.

The main idea is that if technological improvements reduce the unit costs of production, this should be allowed to manifest itself in lower prices.[17]

---

17 Explanations of the Austrian theory of the business cycle typically start with a decline in interest rates, but we could also consider a case where there's an increase in the demand for loanable funds, but the central bank accommodates it with an increase in the money supply such that interest

Dowd (1995) raises some important points about the relationship between agent behaviour and the productivity norm in operation, with regard to the contracts being entered into. He argues that 'we cannot take the contract form as given, and then compare how that fixed contract form performs across two different price-level norms. The choice of contract depends on the norm itself' (ibid.: 721). However, as Selgin (1995: 733) responds, this could be used as a criticism of all price-level norms and therefore does not in itself settle the debate between different ones. Dowd (1995) presents several reasons for favouring price-level stability over a productivity norm, and these include: lower menu costs (the costs of changing nominal prices, such as updating menus); reduced price-level uncertainty; avoidance of indexations costs; increases in productivity; and more macroeconomic stabilisation. He raises critical lines of argument and acknowledges that different price-level norms will score higher on some of these criteria than others. This chapter intends to add three further points of relevance. These are: signal extraction problems; the structure of production; and dangers of over aggregation. We can look at each in turn.

Firstly, signal extraction problems underpin the debate about price-level norms, because even if the price level is 'certain' changes in relative prices can generate miscoordination. Indeed, for the allocation of resources relative prices are more important than the general price level. As

---

rates remain unchanged. In this instance we can see how an Austrian boom piggybacks on a productivity boom.

much of this book argues, the stability of the price level can mask important changes. Dowd (1995) assumes away money illusion but forms of the signal extraction problem may remain. He says, 'under a productivity norm, agents would not know what the price level was likely to be in the aftermath of a major shock. They would therefore have great difficulty setting prices and wages, and the relative price adjustments that must take place would be confused by unnecessary monetary noise' (ibid.: 730). But the 'monetary noise' that prompts signal extraction problems originates from changes in the left side of the equation of exchange, and the impact on the price level (and indeed the price 'swarm') is a consequence.[18]

The second point regards the structure of production. As Selgin (1995: 733) states, the price level means 'an index of prices of final goods'. This demonstrates that a 'price-level norm' is a norm about the level of specific prices – namely output prices. This means that although a price-level norm would leave the *output* price level stable, it would require *factor* prices to adjust (ibid.: 736). By contrast, a productivity norm results in the factor price level being constant, but permits the output price level to change. Dowd (1995: 727) argues, 'since the number of factors is presumably smaller than the number of goods, we must conclude that price-changing costs are lower under price-stability than they are under the productivity norm'. But ultimately it's a

18 Selgin (1995: 735) makes the same point when he says 'it is *not* perfect stability of prices *per se* that is needed to avoid misinterpretation of price signals, but the avoidance of price movements based upon fluctuations in aggregate demand' (emphasis in original).

question of which end of the structure of production you wish to focus on.

The third point is that of over aggregation. Dowd (1995: 723) questions why two parties would want to form contracts that are 'dependent on factors such as economy-wide productivity growth that usually have little or nothing to do with either party'. But the same argument could be used against contracting in terms of output prices, or any other price index.

Perhaps the main argument in favour of a productivity norm, and one that is not dwelled upon by Dowd (1995) or Selgin (1995) is the claim that it mimics a free banking system. Under a productivity norm an increase in Y will cause P to fall. Selgin (1988) provides a theoretical framework to argue that in a free banking system banks will cause M to offset changes in V such that $P + Y$ will remain stable. The problem with a price-level norm is that if Y increases this would require $(M + V)$ to increase. The question is how? Empirically, the question is whether free banking episodes suggest that productivity gains lead to benign deflation as opposed to spontaneous increases in aggregate demand.

Dowd (1995: 730) highlights an apparent inconsistency in Selgin's argument, when he asks 'what magical properties does the productivity norm have that allows inflation to occur without inflation causing any of its usual harm?' The response to this is 'when it is signalling real scarcities'. Dowd's argument is more consistent than Selgin's – inflation is bad regardless of the source. If it's a nominal shock, inflation is bad. If it's a real shock, inflation is bad. Selgin's argument is that inflation is bad when caused by a nominal shock, but good (or at least the lesser of two evils) if caused by a real shock. Indeed, Dowd's argument is not only consistent, it's symmetric. He would argue that deflation is also bad regardless of the source. Selgin is also symmetric – deflation is bad if it's caused by a nominal shock, but good if it's caused by a real shock (i.e. 'benign' deflation).[19]

One of the biggest problems with an inflation target is the fact that real shocks cause monetary policy to be pro-cyclical. As Beckworth and Selgin (2010: 1) say, 'the Fed's occasional, unintentional exacerbation of the business cycle is largely attributable to its failure to respond appropriately to persistent changes in the growth rate of total factor productivity'. By necessity an inflation target entices policymakers to ignore (or at least severely downplay) productivity shocks unless they manifest themselves in changes to consumer prices.[20] In 2005 US policymakers were willing to let real interest rates become negative because easy monetary policy wasn't showing

---

19 It may be worth introducing a Rothbardian voice to the triumvirate. Rothbard, like Dowd, is consistent. He'd argue that inflation is bad regardless of the source. When it comes to deflation Rothbard is consistent in that the source of the shock doesn't matter. But this is asymmetric in that while inflation is bad (regardless of the source), deflation is good (regardless of the source). To clarify, I'm talking about symmetry in terms of real versus nominal shocks, and consistency between inflation and deflation.

20 'The FOMC became increasingly inclined ... to overlook the implications of accelerating productivity growth on the real neutral interest rate, instead preferring to focus on the accelerating growth rate's implications for the rate of inflation' (Beckworth and Selgin 2010).

up in their preferred price index (Beckworth and Selgin 2010):

> [T]he Fed at this date was also aware of increasing symptoms of an overly-easy policy stance, including a weakening dollar and continued housing price inflation. But all such considerations were set aside in favour of an exclusive focus on 'balancing' the risks of inflation and deflation ...

Thus policymakers treat advantageous productivity growth as a sort of free lunch and this makes monetary policy work in the wrong direction:

> [W]hile the tendency of such [productivity] surges to reduce inflation may tempt [policymakers] to set a lower than usual [interest rate] target, theory and prudence call for them to do just the opposite.

Productivity measures are both theoretically and empirically derived from the Solow growth model (Solow 1957), which posits that economic growth is a function of capital and labour. The most common usage of 'productivity' refers to labour productivity – i.e. the quantity of goods and services produced for a given unit of labour (typically hours worked, but also sometimes per worker). It is common to use 'total factor productivity' (TFP) to refer to the part of output growth that is not accounted for by capital or labour (i.e. the Solow residual).[21] In mechanistic terms,

---

21 Traditionally, the Solow residual has been thought of as 'technology', but is now more routinely viewed as a smorgasbord of factors such as managerial competencies, brand management, etc.

TFP is the catch-all category that incorporates additional factors of production. A more nuanced understanding sees TFP as the manner in which capital and labour are combined, or the efficiency with which they are used. One of the charms of using *labour* productivity is the ease of compilation (crudely, the ratio of real output to each labour input). Therefore, while TFP might appear more complete, it is also more controversial. A Bank of England *Quarterly Bulletin* uses a simple Solow model to calculate TFP for 1980–2003 (Groth et al. 2004);[22] however, a few problems emerge. Firstly, their measure of 'capital' derives from a Bank of England working paper (Oulton and Srinivasan 2003) rather than an established data series. Secondly, the share of labour (the exponent within a Cobb–Douglas production function) is assumed to be 0.7, and while this may be in line with reasonable estimations, it is pretty arbitrary.[23] Thirdly, no sensitivity analysis is performed given these assumptions, therefore it is dubious as to how robust the measures are. The authors acknowledge the difficulty in measuring factor inputs, and go on to discuss ways of improving the measures (e.g. using a service measure of capital input rather than stock) and finding new ones (e.g. focusing more on industrial survey data). This underlines the tentative and incomplete nature of data availability.

The Office for National Statistics has provided its own TFP (or multi-factor productivity, MFP) estimates, such as

22 Unfortunately TFP is presented as a chart, and the raw data is not provided.

23 These estimates typically assume that the exponents of both factors sum to one, implying constant returns to scale. Whether this holds at a firm level, economy-wide level and the equivalence of both, is a contentious issue.

Turvey (2009). Unfortunately, this also involves retrospective estimates rather than an updated series. It is also reliant on speculative attempts to measure the capital stock, or what the author refers to as 'experimental estimates of capital services growth' (ibid.: 33). Turvey uses gross value added (GVA) as its measure of output, which ignores much of the productive side of the economy. The author acknowledges this, saying 'including ... intermediate inputs which are omitted from the GVA-based model ... is [conceptually] superior to the one used in this article ... however the data requirements ... are commensurately higher' (ibid.: 34).[24] It is important to note that the alternative being discussed merely breaks the input measures into more categories, but this signals the problems of data availability.

More recently, 2016 saw the publication of MFP estimates from 1971 to 2014 (Blunden and Franklin 2016). These are only available as annual growth rates but we can use them to calculate a multi-factor productivity norm, which is the inflation rate we would observe *if* productivity changes were being reflected. A comparison with CPI is shown in Figure 17.[25]

This implies that productivity gains should have led to a mild deflation all the way from 1997 to 2007, but it also suggests that policymakers should have allowed prices to go higher during the 2008–9 crisis than they did. In 2008

---

24 The European Union includes intermediate inputs such as energy, materials, services in a measure as part of their KLEMS project (see O'Mahony and Timmer 2009).

25 The formula used is simply $PN_t = -PROD_t$.

CPI was 3.6 per cent, but under a productivity norm we might have expected 5.3 per cent.

Figure 17 Actual and multi-factor productivity norm CPI growth, 1997–2014 (annual data, % change from previous year)

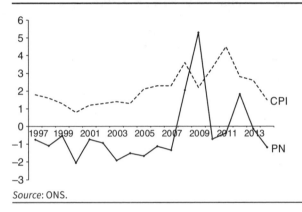

Source: ONS.

In order to use more reliable data (and that which is available quarterly, and for productivity levels rather than growth rates) it is necessary to switch to labour productivity.[26] In the UK, labour productivity (GVA at basic prices divided by hours worked) is a major economic indicator. GDP per hour worked has been a National Statistic since 2006 and is standardised to create International Comparisons of Productivity (ICP) with other G7 countries.

---

26 David Beckworth discusses the difference between a total factor productivity norm and a labour productivity norm. As he points out, the latter will generate a monetary policy rule that results in stable nominal wages, 'but a slightly higher rate of deflation than the total factor productivity norm rule'. This is because nominal income would grow 'at the expected growth rate of labor inputs' (see Beckworth 2007).

Figure 18 shows CPI from 1997 to Q2 2016, alongside the implications of a counterfactual productivity norm.[27] The productivity norm can be used to reveal a 'shadow' rate of inflation that would have transpired if productivity changes had been allowed to affect the CPI.

Figure 18 Actual and productivity norm CPI level, 1997–2016 (quarterly data, 1997 = 100)

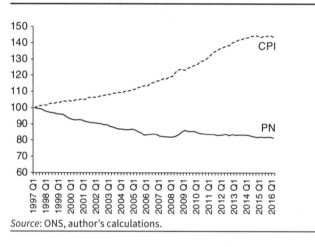

Source: ONS, author's calculations.

Finally, we can also look at the quarterly growth rates using labour productivity. These are shown in Figure 19. This presents a similar picture to the annual figures, and illustrates that since Bank of England independence in 1997, CPI has stayed close to the 2 per cent target. However,

27 The formula used is $PN_t = PN_{t-1} \times (1 + PROD\Delta_t)$, where $PROD\Delta_t = 1 - PROD_t / PROD_{t-1}$.

productivity improvements during this period suggest that without this target CPI should really have been negative for a number of years (i.e. a moderate and mild deflation). This supports the claim that this period had more expansionary monetary policy than is commonly assumed. Indeed, from 1997 to 2007 CPI was on average 3.4 percentage points higher than under a productivity norm benchmark.

Figure 19 Actual and productivity norm CPI growth, 1997–2016 (quarterly data, % change from previous year)

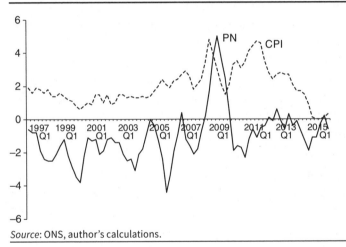

Source: ONS, author's calculations.

Conclusion

Economists are used to describing the period of the Great Moderation as being a success of central bank decision-making. They can successfully point to a record of low and stable inflation. However, this may have been driven by advantageous supply shocks rather than deliberate demand management. And the origins of inflation are important. Credit misallocations can take place under a stable consumer price cover, and looking into what inflation might have been, had productivity improvements been allowed to manifest themselves in a mild deflation, offers a potential source of 'hidden' inflation. In some instances, moderate inflation can be more dangerous than high inflation because it is big enough to cause signal extraction problems, but perhaps not big enough to warrant active attention from economic agents (see Lucas 1975: 1133).

Complaints about official government statistics are common across the world. According to John Williams, the Bureau of Labor Statistics (the US equivalent of the ONS) altered their compilation methods in the 1980s and 1990s in a way that causes CPI to be lower than it otherwise would be. The website gives the impression that the 'shadow' CPI figure is one based on the previous compilation methods. In fact, according to James Hamilton they are simply current CPI data (based on current CPI methods) plus an arbitrary constant.[28] Having presented eight possible sources of the 'hidden inflation' it would be tempting to attempt to draw them together and present a 'real' inflation series. However, it would be a gross oversimplification to make spurious estimates about 'shadow'

---

28 See Aziz (2013). In fact, Hamilton (2008) has quoted Williams as saying the following: 'I'm not going back and recalculating the CPI. All I'm doing is going back to the government's estimates of what the effect would be and using that as an ad factor [sic] to the reported statistics.'

inflation by simply adding constants. Instead, Table 4 presents a simple list with some approximate estimates of the impact. These estimates are applicable to different time periods but they are indicative of a systematic problem.

Table 4   Impact summary

Item	Impact (absolute value)
(i) Compilation error	0.3 per cent
(ii) Changes in target	RPIX was an average of 2.81 per cent from Oct 2002 to Oct 2003 CPI was an average of 1.32 per cent from Nov 2003 to Nov 2004
(iii) Formula effect	0.59 per cent in May 2007 0.77 per cent from May 2007 to May 2014[a]
(iv) Early stage inflation	n/a
(v) Housing costs	0.09 per cent from Jan 2006 to July 2008
(vi) Asset prices	n/a
(vii) Productivity	3.4 per cent
	5.87 per cent[b]

[a] This is the average from May 2007 to May 2014. This will obviously be a more valid estimate of the impact close to this time period.

[b] A rudimentary impact summary can be made by totalling each item. I have taken the difference between RPIX and CPI in item (ii) and the lower bound for item (iii).

This chapter focuses on a key insight, which is that 'a process that deserves to be called "inflationary" may take place under the cover of a "stable" price level' (Marget 1937: 28; see also Marget (1942: 248–49) cited in Egger (1995: 12)). And it has used the search for hidden inflation as a vehicle to provide a critical assessment of various price indices.

The question should not be 'is inflation high?' but 'is inflation higher than it otherwise would be?' We can conclude by saying that Milton Friedman's (1963) classic statement, 'inflation is always and everywhere a monetary phenomenon', requires a companion. This is because, as Niall Ferguson (2006) pointed out:

> There is nothing in Friedman's work that states that monetary expansion is always and everywhere a consumer price phenomenon.

An inflation-targeting regime places a heavy burden on the specific price index being used as the policy target. This chapter has offered several reasons why the CPI has failed, having systematically underreported the inflationary pressure in the UK before the financial crisis. This implies that policymakers should look for a different target. In fact, the argument suggests that they should attempt to target $(P + Y)$ rather than P, and that a level target would be better than a growth target.

5 Y: GDP, GO AND THE STRUCTURE OF PRODUCTION

Summary of key points

- GDP figures available at the time understated the severity of the 2008 recession, but also understated the strength of the recovery.
- GDP is flawed as a measure of well-being, of economic growth, and even of economic activity. We get a fuller picture if we include intermediate consumption (or business-to-business spending), which is known as 'Gross Output' (GO).
- GO for the UK is typically two times bigger than GDP, and more volatile. Unfortunately, official figures are only published on an annual basis, and with a significant lag.

Introduction

GDP figures are as important as they are flawed. For much of 2012 it was believed that the UK had suffered a double dip recession, because the preliminary estimate of 2012 Q1 growth was –0.2 per cent, following growth of –0.3 per cent in 2011 Q4.[1] However, in June 2013 the Q1 figure was revised to 0 per cent growth, thereby eliminating the recession.[2] So much political attention is given to these figures that even movements within the margin of error get reported and latched onto. Throughout the financial crisis, GDP data was misleading in its first release.[3] Major revisions were published in the final estimates of 2011 Q2 (released in September 2011). These were then somewhat offset by corrections made in the final estimate of 2012 Q1 (released in June 2012), and for the 2009 figures in the final estimate of 2013 Q1 (released in June 2013). The key message is that the early estimates of 2008 growth understated the problem.

By contrast, the early estimates of 2009 growth overstated the problem. The first release of 2009 Q1 growth showed that GDP was around –2.0 per cent, but by the end of December 2009 we thought it was worse than –2.5 per cent. In 2011/12 it looked like it was in fact –1.5 per cent, but then in 2013/14 it was revised back down to –2.5 per cent. The other quarters, however, were all ultimately revised up from the earliest estimates. This is in contrast to 2008, where all quarters were revised down. In other words, the crisis was much more severe than we realised at the time, but the recovery was a lot stronger. Using available

---

1   Gross Domestic Product: Preliminary Estimate, Q1 2012, Office for National Statistics, 25 April 2012.

2   Quarterly National Accounts, Q1 2013, Office for National Statistics, 27 June 2013.

3   Revisions triangles for gross domestic product at market prices, chained volume measure. Preliminary Estimates of GDP, Q1 2014.

GDP data for policy decisions meant doing too little too soon, and also too much too late.

When the Quarterly National Accounts were updated in September 2014, even bigger revisions were announced. This was primarily a result of changes to compilation methods, with a reclassification of Research and Development spending and the inclusion of economic activity from the sex and drug industries. The peak-to-trough fall in 2008/09 had previously been estimated to be 7.2 per cent, but this was revised to 6.0 per cent. In fact, Q2 2014 GDP was 2.7 per cent higher than the pre-downturn peak of Q1 2008, having first exceeded this peak in Q3 2013.[4] Ultimately, we discovered that 2012 GDP was 6.2 per cent larger than we'd previously thought (Heath 2014).

Efforts to update the methods introduce new problems either by being incompatible with previous years, or forcing large revisions. In 2014 the Bureau of Economics Analysis (BEA) created a new investment class called 'intellectual property products'. But the type of economic activity that matters is becoming increasingly hard to measure. To what extent is revising GDP compilation methods fighting a losing battle? Is there an alternative?

This chapter attends to the *time structure of production*, building on the work of O'Driscoll and Rizzo (1985), Skousen (1990), Horwitz (2000) and Garrison (2001). These authors all stress two things – that production takes place

---

4 Quarterly National Accounts, Q2, 2014 Office for National Statistics, 30 September 2014.

over time, and that capital goods are heterogeneous.[5] This necessitates shifting attention away from the value of final goods and services (i.e. consumption) and looking at the value of all production. Indeed, when policymakers and commentators focus on 'consumer confidence', they miss the picture – in the words of analyst Sean Corrigan (2007), we need to try 'putting the Hayekian horse [of production] back before the Keynesian cart [of consumption]'. In particular, this chapter applies Skousen's (2010) concept of 'Gross Domestic Expenditure' to the UK economy.[6] It critically assesses the validity of this measure and compares it to other alternatives to GDP such as Rothbard's (1963) 'Private Product Remaining'. Empirical evidence is used to show that the amount of business expenditure far exceeds the amount captured by GDP and is of deep economic significance.[7]

The first section provides an overview of national income accounting and clarifies that we are critiquing GDP on its own terms – as a measure of economic activity. The second section provides a rudimentary look at the potential real GDP growth rate, followed by a critical discussion

---

5 We define the 'time structure of production' as 'an accounting of the pattern and usage of capital goods throughout an entire economy in terms of a value and time dimension' (see O'Driscoll and Rizzo 1985: 166).

6 Skousen (2016) has subsequently adopted the term 'Gross Output' in keeping with the official BEA data series.

7 The main reason why this is so rarely acknowledged comes back to our concept of a time structure of production. In a circular flow that is in equilibrium, the concepts we are discussing are irrelevant. It is only when we view production as a process that takes place over time that we reveal the economic significance of intermediate goods.

of some narrower alternatives to GDP, including Net National Product (NNP) and Net Private Product Remaining (NPPR). The third section looks at the theoretical underpinnings of genuinely *gross* measures of output and why intermediate consumption should be included. It also discusses the release of 'Gross Output' by the BEA. The final section presents a tentative measure of Gross Output for the UK, as well as a look at Total Payments.

National income accounting

In the dynamic equation of exchange, Y refers to the real GDP growth rate. In a real business cycle model with neutral money, the economy will always be in equilibrium and growth will be at potential. We can refer to Y^* as the underlying potential growth rate and use a standard endogenous growth model to understand some of the critical drivers. These include improvements in research and development; better infrastructure; increased competitiveness; higher quality education and training; labour market flexibility; or natural events. Although a discussion of the causes of economic growth is beyond the scope of this chapter, the discipline seems to be taking institutional factors more seriously. The implication of the original Solow growth model is to increase savings and engage in capital accumulation. The implication of endogenous growth theory is to invest in productivity drivers. However, these two aspects of growth, important as they are, are dependent on an appropriate institutional framework. Institutions (the formal and informal rules of the game) cut across the whole economy and determine the effectiveness of innovation. The next section will focus more on capital theory, and this implies that growth is investment led. However, Y^* will be affected by many other issues. For example, in the UK we might point to insufficient immigration; an ageing population; a skills mismatch; technological plateau; eroding competitiveness; reduction in North Sea oil; restrictions on land use; elevated bank capital requirements; increases in regulatory barriers; increase in the size of the state; high marginal tax rates on families with children.[8] Trust in public officials and the independence of the judiciary may be deemed less of a concern, but not all developed countries can take that for granted.

If money is non-neutral, aggregate demand shocks can temporarily move the economy away from Y^*, and hence measured real GDP growth will not provide an accurate estimate.[9] One simple alternative is to rely on productivity data. Figure 20 uses multi-factor productivity as a means of estimating Y^*. This reveals a sharp negative productivity shock in 2008–9 and a subsequent one in 2012.

Before looking at alternatives to GDP, it's important to understand the measure itself and revisit some typical critiques. GDP is an attempt to measure the market value of 'final' goods and services within a particular time period.[10]

---

8   For a further discussion on these themes, see Evans (2014).

9   See Evans (2016b) for a practical demonstration utilising the Dynamic AD-AS model.

10 For a useful overview, see Landefield et al. (2008). For the original, see Kuznets (1934). While GDP tells us the market value of domestically produced final goods and services, Gross National Product (GNP) tells us the

Figure 20 Multi-factor productivity, 1997–2014

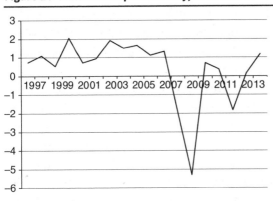

There are three alternative approaches: output, income and expenditure. One of the main differences between them is the speed of data compilation, since the output approach provides the first estimate. Crucially, it is based on the concept of 'value added', which focuses on the difference between gross output and intermediate consumption at each stage of production.[11] The income approach (or GDI) measures the sum of income generated by various groups of producers (for example, corporations, employees, the self-employed). The expenditure approach measures the amount of money spent across all sectors of the economy (i.e. consumption, investment, government spending and net exports). National income accounting is

value of goods produced by residents of that country. For our purposes the two are interchangeable.

11 Note: GDP = Gross value added (GVA) + Taxes – Subsidies.

a relatively new phenomenon and its emergence coincided with the command economy of wartime, because 'planning for the war effort required information on production and spending by type of product and purchaser' (Landefield et al. 2008: 195).

Perhaps the biggest problem with national income accounting is the difficulty in finding a common unit to provide a basis for measurement. Using the cash value of an exchange glosses over the fact that (i) people only exchange when the marginal value is greater than the marginal cost, therefore the exchange price only provides a lower bound of value creation, not an estimate; and (ii) focusing on the monetary value is only a notional measure. The sole reason for engaging in indirect exchange (i.e. using money) is to buy goods and services in the future. Thus, money is merely a 'loose joint' that fails to provide a common unit to compare, for example, apples and pears. The classic critique stems from the originator of national income accounting, with Simon Kuznets famously stating that 'the welfare of a nation [can] scarcely be inferred from a measure of national income' (Kuznets 1934: 7). But we can split these limitations into two separate critiques.

Firstly, there is the critique of GDP *as a measure of well-being*. This is perhaps most commonly encountered in the popular press and stems from the fact that measuring the amount of money spent on goods and services might tell us little about the satisfaction derived from them. Indeed, if human wants can be satisfied better without recourse to economic exchange, then using production as a proxy for well-being is misplaced – production is the necessary prerequisite for consumption and not an end in itself.[12] Not only this, but increased expenditure on some goods might well be a sign of *decreasing* economic well-being – for example, spending on healthcare is a sign of illness. Taking this one step further, if the source of spending is removed from freely consenting consumers (e.g. government spending), it's possible that GDP is reflecting economic *bads* rather than goods. Although this is impossible to objectively measure, some might argue that increases in military spending lead to a reduction in well-being.

GDP also fails to account for externalities. Whereas depreciation of fixed capital can be accounted for, there is no such attention to depreciation of natural resources either through pollution or depletion. While these critiques tend to focus on environmental issues, there is also the source of spending that is important. If consumer spending is financed through credit (either borrowed from overseas or via central bank financed easy money), rather than voluntary savings, this could be unsustainable (Mises 1912; Hayek 1931). Economists who are concerned with asset price bubbles or credit booms would argue

12 A famous joke goes along the following lines: a World Bank consultant takes time out of a conference in an exotic location to take a stroll along the beach. He comes across a young man fishing. He asks whether he has a job and the man replies that all he does is sit on the beach and catch fish. He spends each evening eating under the stars. The consultant suggests that he get a job, and points out that if he works he'll be able to accumulate wealth. 'Why do I need wealth?' 'So that you can save money.' 'Why do I need savings?' 'So that you can build up a pension.' 'Why do I need a pension?' 'So that when you're older you can afford to sit on a beach, catching fish all day, and eating out under the stars.'

that the composition of GDP is more important than the absolute level. And since GDP does not distinguish between real wealth expansion and capital consumption, it masks the most important issue for determining the sustainability of growth.

Secondly, there is the critique of GDP *as a measure of economic activity*. This mainly stems from the fact that an aggregated measure glosses over what the money is being spent on. The quality of goods might be important, since we would expect GDP to be higher if consumers buy cheaper durable goods that need to be replaced more often. Indeed, technological advances might mean that goods and services of higher quality compared with previous time periods become cheaper over time (for example, computers) and bring into circulation products that previously didn't even exist (it is conceptually very hard to make like-for-like living standard comparisons over long periods due to the sheer scale of economic development). Since national accounts are based on survey data, there is also a bias towards existing firms. This is likely to neglect the activity taking place in new firms, which we might expect to be key drivers of growth when the economy is doing well. As Sentance (2012) points out, 'there seems to have been a tendency to underestimate GDP growth when the economy is coming out of recession'.

Many studies attempted to measure the scale of underground economic activity within communist countries, and understandably in contemporary market economies this is assumed to be less of a problem. However, it is easy to think of activities that would constitute 'production' that fail to make it into the national accounts. These might be because they're not exchanged for money (e.g. domestic work, charity work or other unpaid labour) or because they're hidden either for tax avoidance/evasion (e.g. cash-in-hand services, payment in kind) or legal reasons (e.g. illegal but possibly welfare-enhancing trade such as drugs, prostitution or trading by illegal immigrants).

While we would expect subsistence agriculture to be far more prevalent in poorer countries, the scale of childcare and voluntary work in richer countries is vast, and with the rise of free and open-source culture (including software development, music, writing and academic work) could be expanding. Almost by definition the underground economy is hard to measure accurately. However, Fleming et al. (2000) claim that the size of Britain's shadow economy was 13–23 per cent of GDP in 1990–93. Bhattacharyya (2005) finds that the hidden economy accounted for 7–11 per cent of GNP in 1990 (see also Schneider and Enste 2002).

Although GDP does not measure everything that is produced, these standard, well-established textbook criticisms of GDP are usually countered by pragmatism and, while the above problems have validity, they do not necessarily make the construction of economy-wide indicators pointless. Indeed we can take the approach that some forms of aggregate measures might be useful (whether for policymakers, economic forecasters or general business managers), but have more nuanced gripes with the specific composition of GDP. While GDP is a good estimate of national consumption of final goods, it is the desire to dig deeper into the value of intermediate goods that necessitates an alternative.[13]

Beyond GDP

Perhaps one reason why economists and policymakers seem so wedded to GDP is a lack of alternatives. This section attempts to destroy this view by presenting, and critically assessing, several. In particular, we will survey Final Sales, Net National Product (NNP) and (Net) Private Product Remaining (PPR). The subsequent section will be devoted to a discussion of Gross Domestic Expenditure (GDE) and Gross Output (GO).

Selgin (2012) advocates the use of Final Sales of Domestic Product instead of Nominal GDP and there are several advantages. By subtracting inventories, it reveals the amount of spending that takes place in the specific period of observation. By including imports instead of exports, and stripping out inventory accumulation, we see 'what citizens enjoy as opposed to what they produce' (Ranson 2015: 1). Another way of putting this is that it highlights

---

13 The essence of an Austrian approach to measuring output is to draw attention to the entire structure of production, and the discussion that follows will provide the theoretical basis for this view. It will also attempt to relate this to emerging interest from national statisticians, albeit these measures are of nominal output, as opposed to real output. Technically therefore, the remainder of this chapter is looking at the combined growth rate of $(P + Y)$ as opposed to Y. There are two reasons why this is reasonable. Firstly, real GDP is usually calculated by stripping away the effects of inflation, and therefore it's appropriate to start by looking at nominal measures. Secondly, it is only the relatively recent infatuation with delivering constant inflation that creates a large difference between nominal and real measures.

new production as opposed to previous production (in the form of changing inventories). This gives a narrower measure than GDP. Similarly, NNP subtracts depreciation.[14] The downside of this is that the measure of depreciation is an estimate, as opposed to an actual transaction. Therefore, although it may be an important part of the macroeconomic picture, it doesn't tie in closely with monetary theory.[15] In addition, these estimates are based on accounting rather than economic definitions. Even if the concept has more theoretical advantages than GDP, its compilation makes it even harder to use.

The concept of PPR was presented by Rothbard (1963: 224–26, 296–304) as an alternative to GDP, and involves the subtraction of income derived from government sources. Cowen (2014) invokes an NPP argument by advocating an adjustment to GDP that subtracts spending on 'defense or domestic security', 'education' and 'health-care spending'. His rationale is that these are either socially wasteful or intermediate goods, and he points out that their inclusion overstates our measures of national output. He says, 'the narrative of recent U.S. economic history probably would look less promising' (ibid.). This is more of a keyhole approach than Rothbard's since it identifies specific elements of government (and non-government) spending. But the

---

14 According to Munro (2007), this was the measure of national income that Friedman preferred: 'Many have replaced T with Q: the total volume of goods and services produced each year. But the best substitute for T is "y" (lower case Y: a version attributed to Milton Friedman), i.e., a deflated measure of Keynesian Y, as the Net National Product = Net National Income (by definition)'.

15 I thank Robert Thorpe for making this point in via email.

Rothbardian sledgehammer is no better. While measuring government activity at cost undoubtedly inflates GDP figures, disentangling the state is tricky. One rationale is the desire to separate production from transfer payments. But this means that you either claim all government spending is a form of transfer payment (which seems extreme) or neglect that obvious transfer payments (such as unemployment benefits) are already taken out of the government expenditure component of GDP. The next claim is that since government spending must derive from taxation (or future tax obligations) it has already been produced. The problem here is that this argument tends to refer to an infinite time horizon (i.e. spending on a hospital in year t arises from output already created in $t - x$). But GDP is calculated over one year.

The most compelling argument for PPR stems from the 'calculation problem'. Since government spending fails to meet a market test, there is no rationale to determine whether it is genuine production for the sake of want-satisfaction. However, this seems to expose an asymmetry of argument, with the implicit assumption being that non-government spending *does* pass the market test. But we don't have genuinely free markets for anything. The calculation problem doesn't mean that 'private' spending is socially beneficial and 'public' spending is socially detrimental; it means that the larger the size of the state, the harder it becomes to infer consumer satisfaction from economic activity. Consider Cowen (1995):

> Without having access to market prices to evaluate the opportunity costs of resource use, socialist planners

could not tell which outputs should be produced or how to produce them. When it comes to economic value, the socialist planner is literally like the blind man groping in the dark.

We might expect that decisions being made 'in the dark' will be worse than those in the light, but the main point is that we can't tell. The argument for privatising the NHS is not that we know that nurses are social parasites; it's that we don't know what their marginal productivity is. It's quite possible that under a socialised system they receive less than their market wage. We don't know.

Given that libertarians would expect healthcare and education to exist even if they were open to free markets, it's reasonable to infer that some government spending is socially productive. Given that some lawyers wouldn't exist if the economy were more economically liberal, it's reasonable to believe that a lot of 'private' spending is in fact rent seeking.

The real meat of the Austrian justification for PPR seems to be based on libertarian, not economic, reasoning. If you believe that tax is theft, then indeed it seems appropriate to count government spending as categorically different to voluntary spending. In a 1987 article Batemarco (1987) attempted to calculate PPR for the US economy. His justification is as follows:

Because government output is, with few exceptions, not sold on the market, one cannot accurately measure its value. Furthermore, the fact that such output must be financed coercively (through taxation) creates at least a presumption that those unwilling to pay for such output do not place any value on it.

If you take something like healthcare, it seems bizarre that purely because we have a socialised system, we should presume that people place no value on cancer treatment. Also, consider Woods (2008):

> If economists want an idea of the American standard of living today, therefore, or if historians want to uncover its fluctuations over time, both groups are therefore much better served by calculating PPR per capita rather than following the Department of Commerce and its figures for per capita GDP.

He continues, 'The argument that government services, even if coercively funded, may still possess some value, is both raised and answered in Batemarco (1987)'. But Batemarco's treatment of this issue is problematic. Firstly, his claim is only supported by three items of survey evidence. These are: 'Lipset and Schneider cite the median response of people asked what percentage of their tax money is wasted by the federal government to be 48 percent'; 'David Boaz estimates that at least 35 percent of 1982 federal expenditures are of no value to anyone except the special interests which got them enacted in the first place'; and 'The Grace Commission ... was able to find one-third of taxes to be "consumed by waste and inefficiency"'. This hardly constitutes categorical evidence that all public spending is wasteful. The second problem is that he argues that even if government spending is socially useful, it's an intermediate good (and therefore should be stripped out of GDP for risk of double counting). But as we shall see, perhaps intermediate goods *should* be counted.

The purpose of PPR seems to be to counteract the notion that living standards have been steadily rising. Indeed, the fact that the PPR suggests that 'the standard of living for workers in the private sector has been at a standstill since 1964' is evidence for Batemarco that it fits with intuition (although he also offers the possibility that living standards have risen but only because of underground activity). But again, this seems to be a libertarian means to strip out government spending on philosophical grounds, to demonstrate that 'official' figures overstate the productive capabilities of an economy.

Gross production and capital consumption

If we focus on the production approach to national income accounting, and how the 'value added' measure is calculated, an obvious contradiction exists. For example, because 'these gross sales include intermediate sales by businesses to one another' (Landefield et al. 2008: 195), many economists advocate that they be subtracted. This implies that the resulting figure would be a *net* value. Indeed, despite its name, GDP *is* really a net concept, since it subtracts intermediate goods and services that are used in the production of consumer goods.[16] The IMF (1993: 143) defines 'intermediate consumption' thus:

> Intermediate consumption consists of the value of the goods and services consumed as inputs by a process of production, excluding fixed assets whose consumption is recorded as consumption of fixed capital. The goods or services may be either transformed or used up by the production process. Some inputs re-emerge after having been transformed and incorporated into the outputs; for example, grain may be transformed into flour which in turn may be transformed into bread. Other inputs are completely consumed or used up; for example, electricity and most services.[17]

According to Skousen (2016), GO is the value of GDP incorporating intermediate consumption. It is defined as 'the value of all transactions (sales) in the production of new goods and services, both finished and unfinished, at all stages of production inside a country during a calendar year' (Skousen 2010). Intermediate consumption is the means of production, or goods that are 'consumed in the process of further production' (Reisman 1990). Economic

---

16 'GDP is, confusingly, often referred to as net output. To be logically coherent, the "final product" that GDP purports to be should really be defined as the supply of consumer goods plus the change in supply of capital goods' (Reisman 1990). See also Coyle (2014: 7).

17 For our purposes there is no difference between the terms 'intermediate consumption', 'producer goods' or 'capital goods'.

growth requires GO to exceed spending on consumer goods (Phillips et al. 1937: 71–72):

> If real saving is to take place – if the capital equipment of society is to increase – then the gross product of the society very evidently must exceed the amount spent on consumption goods: the gross product must include the amount which makes possible the increase in capital equipment … if all gross income were converted into net income it would mean not only that no progress would be possible, but also that the existing stock of capital goods would not be maintained, and the system would be retrogressive.

The purpose of economic interaction is to satisfy pressing needs, and there are two ways of doing so:

- directly – realising the utility from a good (i.e. 'consumption');
- indirectly – engaging in some form of roundabout method that enables the realisation of greater utility in the future (i.e. 'production').[18]

As John D. Black points out, 'Consumption satisfies human wants directly, and production only indirectly' (Black 1926,

---

18 It's worth pointing out that we only engage in production if it leads to greater consumption. Labour is a 'bad' in the sense that we don't do it for its own sake. In some vocational professions the line may appear blurred, but most people recognise the difference between leisure and work. Note that this supports the common-sense view that wealth accumulation is merely an increase in the stock of capital goods, and that we convert this into utility by consuming the 'consumer' goods that they generate.

cited in Skousen 1990: 96). This distinction, while conceptually stark, is impossible to observe in practice. For example, when Samuelson and Nordhaus (2009) state that bread is a consumer good while wheat is a capital good, in actual fact it depends on their *use*. If the bread were being made into a sandwich prior to consumption, it becomes a capital good. Indeed, *all* goods are merely inputs into psychological want-satisfaction.

In his discussion of the demand for money, Patinkin (1965) argues that whether or not we treat money as a consumption good (in that it generates utility) or a producer good (i.e. an input into the production of consumer goods), matters for welfare economics. He says, 'the treatment of money as a consumer good implies that its services ... should be included in the national product' (ibid.: 160). Since he deems the services that money provides as *not* being a 'final good', 'the contribution of these money services to the total welfare of the economy is already reflected in this output, and it would be "double counting" to include them again' (ibid.: 161). By using a broader measure of national income than GDP, we can avoid some of the tricky task of having to decide whether specific goods are consumer or producer goods. But this implies that we should be seeking a measure of the total capital stock, rather than final goods plus intermediate consumption.

It is also worth commenting on the issue of durability. To talk of 'final goods' implies that they are being consumed and transferred into utility. However, durable goods will be consumed over a long period of time, and while they are being 'consumed' by the 'end user' they are not exhausted. This being the case, it is odd that economists worry so much about the 'exhaustion' of capital goods. For example, 'the argument for the exclusion of intermediate inputs by extension suggests that goods or services sold to consumers for immediate use ... properly belong in GDP' (Hobijn and Steindel 2009: 3). While we may want to capture 'immediate use' and therefore reject capital goods since they tend to be consumed/utilised over several time periods, consistency suggests that we should only focus on *when a good passes through market exchange*, not when it 'releases' utility (ibid.: 4):

> The ambiguities attending the classification of goods as 'final or intermediate' underscore the difficulty of constructing an appropriate measure of GDP. The criteria used to include certain goods and services may not be entirely consistent or clear-cut.

GDP is really an incoherent middle ground. Either it should be a measure of the consumption of final goods (and not include capital goods at all) or incorporate intermediate goods to deliver a measure of the whole capital structure.[19] So GO, like GDP, is a middle ground. But it draws attention

---

19 This point was made to me by Isaac DiIanni, who also points out that the measure of the capital structure depends heavily on institutional factors. It makes little sense, for example, to compare £1 of capital in a socialist economy and £1 of capital in a capitalist economy. While intuitively it seems impossible to measure the entire capital stock, Jeffrey Rogers Hummel has suggested using total net worth (minus human capital) as a reasonable proxy (over email).

to the entire production process, rather than merely the point at which goods reach consumers' hands.

When talking about production, we are talking about entrepreneurship. As previously mentioned, attention to the *heterogeneity* of capital goods leads us down a different path to those who model capital as some homogeneous blob. For example, according to Hobijn and Steindel (ibid.: 3), 'a chip sold to a computer maker, which sells the computer a few days later, is in effect sold twice during a quarter'. But is it the same good? The whole point of entrepreneurship is to create new combinations that *transform* input resources. A chip that is combined with other items is something novel. There is more to a computer than the sum of its parts. Going further, it can be argued that goods gain their economic value when they are made, not when they're exchanged for their market price. According to Horwitz (2000: 180, paraphrasing Hutt):

> [P]roduction takes place not when money is exchanged for an input, but when the input first obtains its market value. For example, acquiring additional education in the hopes of raising one's productivity and one's wages, is an act of production. The exchange of money for services that will follow (if all goes well) is simply turning the productivity into its money's worth; it is not the production itself.

The conception of capital also impacts whether investment is viewed as a gross or net concept. Typically, those who view capital as a perpetual fund take a net approach, whereas a time structure implies gross (Skousen 1990: 19).[20] A gross output approach is therefore concerned with the gross expenditures within an economy. From the perspective of the entrepreneur, the 'value added' is a mysterious phenomena – they need revenues sufficient to cover the *gross* costs of production, and these factor payments are economically relevant. As Skousen (1990: xiv) points out:

> Each firm seeks to maximise net income, but it must raise sufficient capital to finance *gross* expenditures to pay wages, rent, interest, and supplies.

What this relies on is an understanding – one that was prevalent before the Keynesian revolution – that spending on capital goods far exceeds spending on consumer goods. Most economists would acknowledge that intermediate goods are of operational significance to an entrepreneur (Corrigan 2009b: 5), but my point comes from extending this to understand that, although all final goods must derive from intermediate goods, this cannot be glossed over. Corrigan provides a useful analogy. Imagine a fire breaks out and people form a human chain to pass buckets of water along from a water pump to the fire. By only focusing

---

20 Emphasising the Austrian 'gross' approach, 'If entrepreneurs decide not to maintain their capital by not investing enough to enable it to maintain its past output production, then this ... is capital consumption (or disinvestment), even though the physical quantity of capital equipment does not change' (Horwitz 2000: 57).

on final goods, you would be looking at the last man in the chain as they expend the water's use. However, the chain of production is economically significant – there is important economic activity further up the chain, taking place to allow this to happen[21] (Reisman 1990: 677):

> The production of the flour, wheat, and fertilizer are no less real and no less a part of total production than the production of bread; and if they were not produced, bread could not be produced.

The double-counting argument stems from the concern that, since capital goods are bought and sold, including them in the national accounts will overstate the level of production (by incorporating the same goods being traded over different time periods). However, this also rests on an assumption that the total value of final goods will equal the combined value of all component parts. This issue can be traced back to Adam Smith and is of seminal importance to how we understand economic production. According to Smith (1776, book 2, ch. 2: 88):

> The value of the goods circulated between the different dealers, never can exceed the value of those circulated between the dealers and the consumers; whatever is bought by the dealers, being ultimately destined to be sold to the consumers.

---

21 It's worth pointing out that economic forecasters tend to focus on indicators upstream at the 'production' end of the economy rather than downstream at the consumer end.

Part of the problem is that this rests on the labour theory of value, and the assumption that the cost of production determines the final value of a consumer good. In reality, the price is reflection of both the cost of production *and* the subjectively determined marginal value; therefore intermediate goods are not necessarily counted. Indeed, F. A. Hayek – building on the work of Carl Menger that treated production as a temporal process – grasped this point[22] (Hayek 1931: 235):

> [T]his proposition clearly rests upon a mistaken inference from the fact that total expenditure made in production must be covered by the return from the sale of the ultimate products ... the solution of the difficulty is, of course, that most goods are exchanged several times against money before they are sold to the consumer, and on the average exactly as many times as often as the total amount spent for producers' goods is larger than the amount spent for consumers' goods.

Even if we grant the use of the term 'gross' domestic product to apply to a fundamentally 'net' concept, by insisting on looking at 'final goods' solely, we see some bizarre arguments. The implication, as Reisman (1990) points out, is that the final product is *equal* to the total product: that bakers do not produce bread, but the difference between

---

22 Similarly, 'capital goods ... derive their value from the value of their prospective products; nevertheless, their value never reaches the full value of those prospective products, but as a rule remains somewhat below it' (Mises 1912: 339).

flour and bread. That the bread is *actually* produced by their suppliers, and the baker is actually producing 'conceptual differences'. The confusion stems from the fact that production takes place in different stages (i.e. over time). In actual fact (Phillips et al. 1937: 70):

> [I]t is not even necessary that the current money income of consumers should be equal to the net product produced, because of corporate and other business savings used to maintain and replace the existing stock of capital goods. Therefore, the net income in the form of money payments to *consumers* neither ordinarily will nor should be great enough to enable them to command the entire gross product of industry.[23]

Finally, if one were really concerned about double counting, then why include capital goods at all? Reisman (1990) makes the claim that standard GDP accounting involves double counting even when ignoring intermediate consumption. This is because it is somewhat arbitrary as to which capital goods are treated as intermediate goods.

Skousen (2013) makes a distinction between the 'make' economy, which includes 'the supply chain and intermediate stages of production required to produce all the finished goods and service', with the 'use' economy, which is those finished goods and services. He points out that most leading economic indicators focus on early stages

---

23 In other words, it is only necessary that it covers the current production of final consumer goods.

of production and that GDP under-represents the amount of economic activity taking place. As Hanke (2014) says, 'consumption is not the big elephant in the room. The elephant is business expenditures'. Indeed, in April 2014 the BEA began to release estimates of GO on a quarterly basis (see Skousen 2014 for more details). Conceptually, we can treat GO as a movement towards the full productive economy.

Figure 21 Structure of production

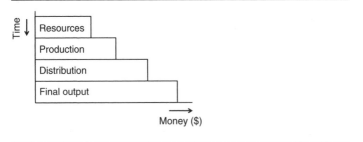

Consider the structure of production depicted in Figure 21 (see Hayek 1935; Skousen 1990; Garrison 2001). The y-axis shows time, with more distant stages of production further away from the origin. The x-axis shows the monetary value of the activity that is taking place. A conventional approach is to look at various 'intermediate' stages of production, such as mining, manufacturing and wholesale. These all lead towards the final stage of production, i.e. retail. In the version above, the aim is to tie into National Accounts, and we can use this as a basis to consider two common ways to measure GDP. The expenditure approach looks at final output alone.

The value-added approach looks at the first stage and then the sum of the difference between each subsequent stage. Figure 22 shows why these should deliver the same estimate.[24]

Figure 22 Structure of production (GDP)

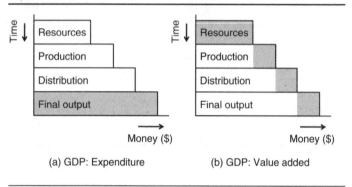

(a) GDP: Expenditure   (b) GDP: Value added

We can also use these 'Hayekian' triangles to show the GO measure (Figure 23). GO is the sum of intermediate consumption and GDP, but since this only measures wholesale/distribution and retail trades/final output at the margin, additional adjustments are required to compile Gross Domestic Expenditure (GDE).[25]

The findings are important. Corrigan (2009b: 6) shows that if US Gross Domestic Output is adjusted for imports, 'while the official Nominal GDP number came in at $13.4 trillion, business spending amounted to more

---

24 These are based on Skousen (2010).

25 Or 'Adjusted' Gross Output. See Skousen (2016) for more details.

than \$31 trillion, around 2⅓ times bigger'. According to Skousen (2014):

> [I]n 2008–09, nominal GDP declined only 2% while nominal gross output fell sharply by 8%, far more indicative of the depths of the recession. Interestingly, since the 2009 trough, gross output has been rising faster than GDP, suggesting a more robust recovery.

Figure 23 Structure of production (GO)

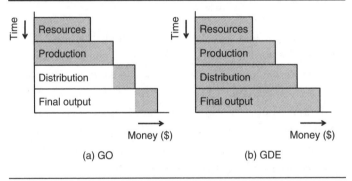

Geloso (2015; 2016) also found that prior to 2008 nominal GO grew more rapidly than nominal GDP, but then fell more dramatically in 2008–9. More recently, Hanke (2014) reports that in 2013 GO was 76.4 per cent larger than GDP, while GDE was 120.4 per cent larger. And Ranson (2015) provided tentative evidence that that since 1997 real GO was better correlated with financial-price movements than real GDP.

Evidence for the UK economy

This section intends to present evidence that allows us to go beyond GDP and factor in the productive side of the UK economy. In particular, it will present a new time series of GO and present estimates of total transactions.

GO is compiled using input–output data and is released as part of the 'Supply and Use tables'. It is equal to the sum of total intermediate consumption and nominal GDP. According to the Office for National Statistics (Drew and Dunn 2011):

> The Supply and Use tables are compiled around 18 months after the year in question, when comprehensive information on expenditure, income and production becomes available. The expenditure, income and production approaches are based on different survey and administrative data sources and each produces estimates that are subject to uncertainty. Accordingly, the three approaches produce different estimates, although theoretically they should be the same. A single, definitive, GDP estimate can only emerge therefore after a process of balancing and adjustments.

Not only are the data published with an 18 month lag, they are only available on an annual basis.[26] This is in stark

---

26 There are two spreadsheets that are released containing the information. In one of them, there isn't even a time series available. Therefore, the data presented here are based on copying from each tab and pasting into a new series. It is usually released on the last day of July each year. The figures

contrast to GDP, which gets revised three times and up-dated every quarter. As we've seen, however, this availabil-ity of GDP data may be part of its downfall.

In 2014 nominal GDP was £1.82 trillion while GO was £3.34 trillion (Figure 24). In 1997 GO was 1.8 times as large as GDP, and this ratio fell to 1.78 in 2005. As Figure 25 shows, it rose to 1.85 times in 2009.

When combined with similar studies in the US, it seems reasonable to adopt this as a rule of thumb – that includ-ing intermediate consumption *doubles* the measure of economic activity, and that this reduces substantially the importance of final consumption. Indeed, this discussion has serious implications for the contemporary use of fiscal policy. If 70 per cent of GDP is consumption, this encour-ages policymakers to believe (falsely) that consumption drives aggregate demand (i.e. boosting consumption is the key to the recovery). In actual fact, production is a far greater part and *entrepreneurs* are the 'prime movers'.[27]

And not only is it bigger, it might be more *volatile*. It is fairly conventional wisdom that investment spending tends to be more volatile than consumer spending,[28] and thus focusing on consumer spending and consumer prices severely underestimates the flux of the economy. Skousen

---

used here were released on 29 July 2016. Nominal GDP data are taken from the Second Estimate of Q2 2016, released on 26 August 2016.

27 Consumer confidence is thus largely passive compared to what's going on within the real economy.

28 'It is a universally recognised fact that during the course of the business cycle the capital goods industries tend to fluctuate much more violently than do those industries which produce for current consumption' (Ham-berg 1951, cited in Skousen 1990: 304).

(1990) cites a study showing that, during the Great Depression, 'personal consumption expenditures declined from $77 billion to $46 billion, a 40 percent reduction. Meanwhile, capital investments declined more steeply, from $16 billion to $1.4 billion, a collapse of over 90 percent' (US Department of Commerce 1975). For historical studies that lend empirical support to the notion that prices in sectors further away from consumption fluctuate by more than those relatively closer, see Estey (1950) and Mills (1946) (cited in Skousen 1990: 291).

Figure 24 GO vs NGDP, 1997–2014 (£million)

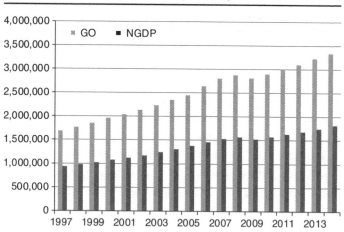

The main difference between nominal GDP and GO can be seen by comparing the growth rates, as in Figure 26. In 2002 the growth rate of NGDP began to accelerate beyond that of GO, hitting a peak of 5.95 per cent in

2003 (compared to 4.82 per cent). Then, in 2006, although the NGDP growth rate remained fairly stable (at 5.52 per cent as compared to 5.72 per cent in 2005), the GO growth rate jumped from 4.21 per cent in 2005 to 7.88 per cent in 2006. This large increase in economic activity immediately before the financial crisis might have served as a warning sign, were it available. This also reveals a limitation of annual data because the crisis began in earnest in the middle of 2008. Therefore, the 2008 GO growth rate of 2.5 per cent captures part of the boom and part of the bust. Both growth rates have been weaker after the crisis than before.

Figure 25 GO to NGDP ratio, 1997–2014

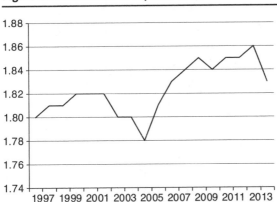

Over the years where data are available (1997–2014), GO has a standard deviation 1.83 times greater than GDP. There is weak support for the theoretical premise that GO fluctuates by more than NGDP.

For all that has been said about the importance of production, entrepreneurs are only responding to the (often unarticulated) desires of consumers, hence 'the continually changing demands for consumer goods imply a continuing revaluation in the capital goods used in their production' (O'Driscoll and Rizzo 1985: 161). Consequently, we'd expect the 'heavy lifting' of economic adjustments to occur in those industries and for those goods relatively far from immediate exhaustive consumption.

Figure 26 GO and NGDP growth, 1998–2014

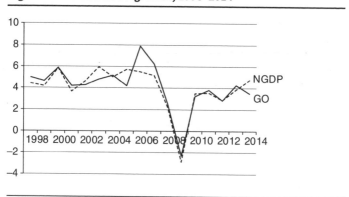

Corrigan (2009b: 6) finds that 'the volatility [of business expenditures] is 5.3 and its range stretches no less than 5.7 sigmas … the latter's volatility [of exhaustive consumption] is a much lesser 2.3 and encompasses only a 3.7 sigma range' (ibid.: 1):

As the Austrian model tells us, just like specialized predators in an ecological system, the makers of 'higher-order' goods are uniquely vulnerable to a recessionary wave, no matter where or how it originates, thanks to a combination of the elevated degree of specificity in their capital equipment and their almost complete reliance on those highly discretionary outlays which emanate from further down the structure of production where more flexibility is often employed.

Ultimately, however, all GO does is bring us closer to total transactions.[29] As Congdon (2012: 6) says, 'No exact quantification of this supposed "T" has ever been attempted'. However, we can make an approximation using payments data. The UK Payments Council reports the transactions that take place via different payments systems. These include Bacs, CHAPS, Faster Payments and Cheque & Credit Clearing Company (C&CCC).[30] They reveal not only total business receipts, but also consumer spending. Despite flaws in the data we can see several important things.[31] Figure 27 shows payment growth from 1990 to 2013 and Figure 28 shows the annual growth rate.

---

29 Indeed, I am using $M + V = P + Y$ as the central organising principle because the aim of this work is to contribute to current policy debate, and following Friedman, Y is more readily available. But if the goal is to create a stable 'total income stream', this implies that the right-hand side should be $(P + T)$. I believe it is appropriate to treat GO as an alternative measure of output (Y), rather than an estimate of transactions (T). But the purpose of this chapter is to bridge the gap.

30 The spreadsheet is called 'Historical Monthly Statistics (1990 to date)' and is available at http://www.paymentscouncil.org.uk/resources_and_publications/publications/reports/#anchor5 (accessed 1 August 2014).

31 For example, for some reason a figure for January 2010 is missing.

Figure 27 UK payments, 1990–2013 (2006 = 100)

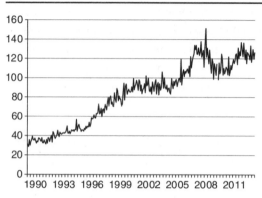

Figure 28 UK payments growth (% change on previous year)

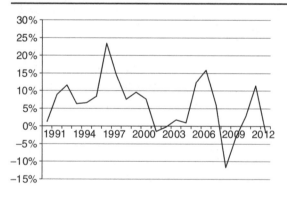

We can also compare total payments with broad monetary aggregates. According to Congdon (2012), bank lending to the private sector was +£235.8 billion in 2006 and –£164.1 billion in 2010. However, total UK payments in 2012 were £75,000 billion. As he says, 'the proportion of total transactions financed by new bank lending is trivially small'. According to the figures used above, from 2012 to 2013 total payments were on average 3.87 times the size of M4ex. The fact that total payments dwarf bank lending casts doubt on the idea that the latter somehow drives economic recovery. But also note that if we move all the way to attempting to measure transactions, it will comprise mostly financial market transactions, and the real economy would be almost irrelevant (see Sumner 2016).

Conclusion

This chapter seeks to provide a better impression of the economy by modifying the measures of national income. This involves the incorporation of the productive sectors of the economy and avoiding the false assumption that this always shows up in final consumer goods. GDP is a useful measure that captures a large part of economic activity and provides a meaningful gauge of human flourishing. But when judged on either criteria it has serious limitations. The elevated status it has achieved as a focal point for media attention is problematic, as its chief historic significance has been as solution to a problem only created by central planning and an attempt to utilise macroeconomic variables for policy goals. Greater attention to alternative indicators – such as Gross Output and Total Payments – not only permits a more coherent understanding of macroeconomic performance, but also broadens the range of criteria on which the meddler could be judged.

Indeed, recent changes to the composition of GDP have dramatically changed our understanding of the economic recovery and would have almost certainly implied an alternative policy response. A chief advantage of GO is that by incorporating intermediate consumption it is more robust to compilation changes. And given that difficult decisions about what constitutes intermediate, as opposed to final, consumption are likely to increase in future (Coyle 2014), GDP will lose relevance.

Ultimately, we could have a spectrum with consumption at one end and the entire capital stock at the other. Both of these provide coherent measures. GDP falls somewhere towards consumption and GO moves us closer to the capital stock. The first step towards a fruitful conversation about alternatives to GDP is improvement in statistical reporting.

6 CONCLUSION

One of my favourite works of pop science is David Bodanis's 2001 book, $E = mc2$. It is well researched, beautifully written and has a majestic organising principle – each chapter is devoted to a different component of Einstein's most famous equation. I have long since felt that the equation of exchange, upon which the quantity theory is built, warrants similar treatment. Indeed, Milton Friedman once remarked that 'Fisher's equation [$MV = PT$] plays the same foundation-stone role in monetary theory that Einstein's $E = mc2$ does in physics' (van Overtveldt 2007: 166). However, as Congdon (2011: 316) has pointed out, the analogy shouldn't be taken too far: 'the trouble with this sort of assertion was that it overlooked that money and banking are human institutions, and the way in which people use their media of exchange is always changing'. By treating each element in isolation, and assessing their usefulness as indicators, we run the risk of forgetting that what really matters is how they interact, and that this is driven by human action. So this conclusion will be split into two parts. Firstly, I will discuss the dynamic process of economic crises, focusing on the interaction between different variables.[1] Secondly, I will outline some broad policy conclusions.

The dynamic process of economic crises

To look in more depth at economic crises we can consider two forms: inflationary booms and deflationary spirals. In terms of inflation, if the growth of the money supply exceeds the growth of real output, then inflationary pressure will occur. The direct channel leads to a consumption boom, and the indirect channel leads to an investment boom. Both are unsustainable. The Austrian theory of the trade cycle (Mises 1912; Hayek 1931; Garrison 2001) explains the upper limit: economic growth is constrained by the pool of real savings. If the money supply grows by too much, then a crisis is inevitable. Hyperinflation – which ultimately is a complete breakdown in the monetary system – is the potential consequence of not facing up to this reality.

When it comes to deflation, one often encounters an asymmetric concern. A general view is that, while monetary expansions are controllable, monetary contractions are not (Simons 1938: 222):

> Once a deflation has gotten under way, in a large modern economy, there is no significant limit which the decline in prices and employment cannot exceed, if the central

---

1   Evans (2016) shows how the dynamic AD-AS model can be used as a pedagogical tool and simple policy framework that draws together the components of the equation of exchange.

government fails to use its fiscal powers generously and deliberately to stop the decline. Only great government deficits can check the hoarding of lawful money and the destruction of money substitutes once a general movement is under way.

Therefore, the threat of deflation is given far greater prominence than the threat of inflation. But first it is crucial to make a distinction between price deflation and monetary deflation. As Hayek says, 'that there is no harm in prices falling as productivity increases has been pointed out again and again' (Hayek 1931: 284), and he cites the likes of Marshall, Edgeworth, Pigou and Robertson. The argument is highly intuitive – since we value present consumption greater than distant consumption, we're willing to pay a premium to bring consumption forward. The promise of lower prices in the future is therefore hardly reason for the indefinite postponement of gratification. It is the primary purpose of the capitalist process to make goods and services cheaper over time. Indeed, the empirical evidence finds no real correspondence between deflation and economic depressions, 'in a broader historical context, beyond the Great Depression, the notion that deflation and depression are linked virtually disappears' (Atkeson and Kehoe 2004). Thus we need to focus our concerns on a monetary contraction.

The most famous 'process' account of deflation is Irving Fisher's theory of 'debt-deflation' (Fisher 1933), but he was far from being the only 'classical' quantity theorist that provided a dynamic account (for example, Machlup

1935, or a Wicksellian 'cumulative rot'). In short, if debt contracts are fixed in nominal terms, then falling prices increase the real debt burden, and 'the very effort of individuals to lessen their burden of debts increases it, because of the mass effect of the stampede to liquidate in swelling each dollar owed ... the more the debtors pay, the more they owe' (Fisher 1933: 344). This can have a cumulative effect throughout the economy as a whole. Fisher (ibid.: 342) provides nine 'links' to the crisis, but consider 3, 4 and 5:

> (3) a fall in the level of prices ... (4) a still greater fall in the net worths of business, precipitating bankruptcies and (5) a like fall in profits.

Here, Fisher seems to be misguided by the aggregation that the quantity theory encourages. It is not necessarily the case that falling prices lead to bankruptcies, since this depends on whether input prices are falling faster than consumer prices. Link number 7 is 'pessimism and loss of confidence'. This brings us back to the demand for money, and how increases (for example, as the consequence of a panic) can cause prices to fall. An 'excess' demand for money exists when an ex ante desire for cash balances exceeds the actual cash balance, leading to the inverse of an inflationary boom. Instead of people spending their excess money, they offload their excess goods and services. Both actions are governed by a desire for monetary equilibrium. But if the supply of money hasn't risen accordingly, this fire sale will depress prices. If we make the plausible claim that the demand for money is driven largely by uncertainty and that uncertainty increases during a panic, we begin to see a causal process emerge. However, this is not known a priori. It is also possible that the public are already concerned about the level of personal debt and foresee a correction. The culmination of this might lead to a 'clean break' that allows confidence to begin an economic recovery. For example, sovereign debt crises do not necessarily lead to prolonged crises, and getting it over with quickly might be a faster route to recovery overall. The bottom line is that debt-deflation is one possible outcome of a monetary deflation, and it is applicable when there are high levels of debt and there is no reflation. Similarly, the Austrian theory of the inflationary boom is applicable when it is a credit-fuelled cycle.

According to Horwitz, 'if there are sound reasons to believe prices cannot react instantaneously, then the costs are real' (Horwitz 2006: 171) and, as already discussed, most economists acknowledge the real world presence of various forms of price rigidity. Just as the boom creates misallocations of capital, the crash means that capital isn't allocated at all. Instead of the 'forced saving' caused by capable entrepreneurs priced out of the market, we see that 'forced investment', in the form of 'unsold inventories on store shelves will be the manifestation of the reverse form of intertemporal discoordination. Producers continue to produce for a level of consumption that is no longer relevant' (Horwitz 2006). Ultimately, the disruption to relative prices during the boom is compounded by a further disruption during the crash.

Policy conclusions

Before adopting quantitative easing, in 2009, the Bank of England's Monetary Policy Committee (MPC) had a pretty simple remit. Their sole target was to achieve 2 per cent inflation, and their only tool was interest rates. This hadn't always been the case, and other central banks generally followed a similar trend. Under the Bretton-Woods system, countries were committed to fixing their exchange rate to the price of gold. But when this collapsed in the 1970s, central banks had more opportunity to use monetary policy to meet other targets. Espousing the dominant Keynesian appetite for managing the economy, there was an eclectic combination of goals, from domestic prices to exchange rates to unemployment.

The perceived breakdown of the Keynesian system came with the stagflation of the late 1970s, and this coincided with Milton Friedman's identification of the historic link between the money supply and inflation. The basic monetarist tenet that velocity and real growth were reasonably stable (or at least offset each other) implied that to control inflation you need only focus on controlling the money supply. This led to a trend towards money growth rules and attention to monetary aggregates. By the 1990s, however, it is generally accepted that financial innovations altered the demand for money and, thus, velocity became volatile. The New Keynesian school combined two key things. The first is the importance of expectations. The argument is that if the only thing that central banks can ultimately control is inflation, provided they can keep inflation expectations anchored at a low, stable rate, people can plan effectively and everything else will fall into line. The second was an emphasis on the short-term interest rate as the most timely and easy-to-monitor way to conduct monetary policy. Thus central banks moved away from a money growth target and towards an inflation target. Since the 2008 financial crisis, central banks have evolved further. They now give increased consideration to whether inflation is the right target after all, and reaching the zero lower bound has prompted a return to controlling the money supply directly (i.e. quantitative easing). These tweaks to the status quo have thus far failed to turn into a new framework, and exist as a hodgepodge of experiments. A contributor to the financial crisis, however, has been inflation targeting, and it needs to be replaced.

The main criticism of inflation targets is that, in certain circumstances, they give rise to counterintuitive policy decisions. For example, if a negative supply shock coincides with a weakening economy, this will cause inflation to rise and be a signal to an inflation-targeting central bank to tighten policy. However, this will only reinforce the weakness. Advocates of an inflation target would say that in such circumstances – and the summer of 2008 is a prime example – they should 'see through' the price spikes. But it can be difficult to know whether inflation is driven by demand or supply side shocks. Therefore, a third option would be to say that as long as nominal income is stable, people can form expectations, but inflation can do its job of altering in response to changes in productivity and the productive capacity of the economy.

If we return to the dynamic equation of exchange, recollect that the combined growth rate of the money supply and velocity of circulation will be equal to the combined growth rate of inflation and real output growth:

$$M + V = P + Y.$$

We can see three clear implications for monetary policy. The first is to target M. The second is to target P. The third is to target $P + Y$.

A nominal income (or NGDP) target would require that the monetary authority adjusts M in response to changes in V, in an attempt to mimic a neutral monetary system which would 'stabilise' $M + V$. When economists warn about the inflationary tendencies of central banks and the dangers of generating an artificial boom, we can make a distinction between two phases of the crisis. It is dangerous for central banks to expand the money supply beyond the demand to hold cash balances, but if this has already happened, it is also dangerous to fail to respond to an increase in the demand for money. According to Lachmann (1978: 120):

> [W]here the banks are involved ... the danger of a *secondary deflation* is always present. When that happens the 'recession' which succeeded the strong boom will turn into a 'depression', a cumulative process of income contraction, as has often happened in the past. Of course it need not happen. But to avert the danger must always be the primary aim of monetary policy in a recession.

Egger (1995) explains how this secondary deflation occurs. The primary deflation causes prices to fall, and if people expect this to continue their demand for cash balances will rise and thus velocity falls. All else equal, the fall in velocity would cause prices to fall even further. Monetary authorities can attempt to remedy this by increasing the supply of money to accommodate the increased demand to hold it. Policymakers can verify if they are succeeding by looking at whether or not nominal income is contracting.

As already discussed, however, those indicators are not necessarily available. The measure of P should contain asset prices and we also need a broader measure of economic activity than GDP. However, we don't have accurate measures of total transactions and efforts to capture more of the structure of production (such as GO) come with a significant lag. Even more critically, the incentive systems and knowledge processes within a banking system with a central bank are vastly different from what would occur in a free banking regime. As Salter (2013) has said, there's a world of difference between saying, 'in a free banking environment the private banking system would adjust M to offset changes in V, such that $P + Y$ is stable' and 'the central bank should target $P + Y$'.

In Evans (2016a) I provide a fuller proposal for an NGDP target, as well as arguing that its primary advantage is its potential to serve as a stepping-stone to the ultimate goal of free banking. For now, however, if the immediate goal is to improve central banking, we can summarise with the following key implications:

- We should pay more attention to monetary aggregates and, in particular, new measures such as MA and Divisia money, as early-warning indicators.
- Central banks should be careful not to damage confidence by creating regime uncertainty, but should be ready to accommodate changes in velocity.
- We should pay more attention to inflation measures that include asset prices, and replace inflation targeting with a nominal GDP level target.
- Where possible, GO should be used as a complement to GDP to get a better understanding of economic activity throughout the entire structure of production.

REFERENCES

Alchian, A. A. and Klein, B. (1973) On a correct measure of inflation. *Journal of Money, Credit and Banking* 5(1):173–91.

Aldrick, P. (2012) Inflation change could deliver £3bn windfall. *Daily Telegraph*, 18 September.

Artus, P. (2015) What is the link between monetary policy, the money supply and inflation? Natixis Economics Research no. 863.

Atkeson, A. and Kehoe, P. J. (2004) Deflation and depression: is there an empirical link? *American Economic Review*, Papers and Proceedings 94(2): 99–103.

Aziz, J. (2013) The trouble with shadowstats. Azizononomics, 1 June, http://azizonomics.com/2013/06/01/the-trouble-with-shadowstats/ (accessed 27 March 2015).

Bank of England (2011) Quarterly Bulletin 2011 Q1.

Bank of England (2013) Bank of England and *The Times* Interest Rate Challenge 2013/14. London.

Barnett, W. A. (1980) Economic monetary aggregates: an application of aggregation and number index theory. *Journal of Econometrics* 14(1): 11–48.

Barnett, W. A. (2012) *Getting It Wrong: How Faulty Monetary Statistics Undermine the Fed, the Financial System, and the Economy.* Cambridge, MA: MIT Press.

Barnett, W. A. and Chauvet, M. (2011) How better monetary statistics could have signalled the financial crisis. *Journal of Econometrica* 161(1): 6–23.

Batemarco, R. (1987) GNP, PPR, and the standard of living. *Review of Austrian Economics* 1: 181–86.

BBC (2011) We will 'get tough' on excessive boardroom pay – Clegg. BBC News, 4 December.

Beckworth, D. (2007) A brief look at the productivity norm rule. Macro and Other Market Musings, 23 September, http://macromarketmusings.blogspot.co.uk/2007/09/mark-toma-points-us-to-knzn-who-is.html (accessed 2 April 2015).

Beckworth, D. (2009) Does the equation of exchange shed any light on the crisis? Macro Musings Blog, 17 September, http://macromarketmusings.blogspot.co.uk/2009/09/does-equation-of-exchange-shed-any.html.

Beckworth, D. (2011a) Taking seriously the excess money demand problem: a reply to Robert Murphy. Mises Wire, 18 January, https://mises.org/wire/taking-seriously-excess-money-demand-problem-reply-robert-murphy.

Beckworth, D. (2011b) FOMC: we got a money demand problem. Macro Musings Blog, 12 October, http://macromarketmusings.blogspot.co.uk/2011/10/fomc-we-got-money-demand-problem.html (accessed 8 July 2014).

Beckworth, D. (2013) The low-interest-rate blues. *National Review*, 30 May, http://www.nationalreview.com/article/349636/low-interest-rate-blues-david-beckworth (accessed 8 July 2014).

Beckworth, D. and Selgin, G. (2010) Where the Fed goes wrong: the 'productivity gap' and monetary policy. Working Paper.

Belongia, M. T. (1996) Measurement matters: recent results from monetary economics reexamined. *Journal of Political Economy* 104(5): 1065–83.

Belongia, M. T. and Ireland, P. N. (2010) The Barnett Critique after three decades: a New Keynesian analysis. *Journal of Econometrics* 183(1): 5–21.

Belongia, M. T. and Ireland, P. N. (2014) Interest rates and money in the measurement of monetary policy. *Journal of Business and Economic Statistics* 33(2): 255–69.

Begg, D., Fischer, S. and Dornbusch, R. (2008) *Economics*, 9th edn. New York: McGraw-Hill.

Bernanke, B. (1983) Irreversibility, uncertainty and cyclical investment. *Quarterly Journal of Economics* 98(1): 85–106.

Bhattacharyya, D. (2005) On the estimation and updating of the hidden economy estimates: the UK experience. In *Size, Causes and Consequences of the Underground Economy: An International Perspective* (ed. C. Bajada and F. Schneider). Aldershot: Ashgate.

Black, J. D. (1926) *Introduction to Production Economics*. New York: Henry Holt.

Blunden, A. and Franklin, M. (2014) Multi-factor productivity estimates: Experimental estimates to 2014. Office for National Statistics.

Bodanis, D. (2001) $E = mc^2$: *A Biography of the World's Most Famous Equation*. New York: Berkley.

Böhm-Bawerk, E. (1891) *The Positive Theory of Capital*. London: Macmillan.

Brown, D. (2013) Money beats credit (and especially, Divisia money). Wonkery, 5 October.

Brummer, A. (2009) *The Crunch: How Greed and Incompetence Sparked the Credit Crisis*. London: Random House.

Buiter, W. (2009) Quantitative and qualitative easing again. *Financial Times*, 11 January.

Burgess, S. and Janssen, N. (2007) Proposals to modify the measurement of broad money in the United Kingdom: a user consultation. *Bank of England Quarterly Bulletin* Q3: 402–14.

Cannan, E. (1921) The meaning of bank deposits. *Economica* 1(1): 28–36.

Carlson, J. B. and Keen, B. D. (1996) MZM: a monetary aggregate for the 1990s? *Federal Reserve Bank of Cleveland, Economic Review* 32(2): 15–23.

Christensen, L. (2012) Regime uncertainty, the Balkans and the weak US recovery. The Market Monetarist, 31 October.

Christensen, L. (2013) The (Divisia) money trail – a very bullish UK story. The Market Monetarist, 9 December.

Cocozza, P. (2012) What can you pay for with 1p and 2p coins? Not an £800 bill... *The Guardian*, 15 May.

Cohen, N. (2009) Money supply supplants rates on Bank's agenda. *Financial Times*, 6 April.

Coletti, D., Lalonde, R. and Muir, D. (2008) Inflation targeting and price-level-path targeting in the global economy model: some open economy considerations. *IMF Staff Papers* 55(2): 326–38.

Congdon, T. (1995) Broad money vs. narrow money. *Review of Policy Issues* 1(5): 13–27.

Congdon, T. (2007) Special report: broad money vs. narrow money. Lombard Street Research, 4 April.

Congdon, T. (2011) *Money in a Free Society: Keynes, Friedman, and the New Crisis in Capitalism*. New York: Encounter Books.

Congdon, T. (2012) Weekly email, 3 October.

Consumer Reports (2012) Many common medical tests and treatments are unnecessary. June.

Cookson, P. (2014) Does the VIX really measure volatility? FT Alphaville, http://ftalphaville.ft.com/2014/06/20/1882462/guess -post-does-the-vix-really-measure-volatility/ (accessed 10 July 2014).

Coppola, F. (2013) There's a problem with the transmission... Coppola Comment, 31 May.

Corrigan, S. (2007) Putting the Hayekian horse back before the Keynesian cart. Safehaven, 27 March, https://safe haven.com/article/7169/putting-the-hayekian-horse-back -before-the-keynesian-cart.

Corrigan, S. (2009a) The descent of man. Diapason Research Report, April.

Corrigan, S. (2009b) Bastiat's iceburg. Diapason Research Report, December.

Cowen, T. (1995) A review of G. C. Archibald's information, incentives, and the economics of control. *Journal of International and Comparative Economics* 4: 243–49.

Cowen, T. (2014) *GDP: A Brief But Affectionate History* by Diane Coyle and *The Leading Indicators: A Short History of the Numbers That Rule Our World* by Zachary Karabell. *Washington Post*, 21 February.

Coyle, D. (2014) *GDP: A Brief But Affectionate History*. Princeton University Press.

Cronin, D. and Dowd, K. (2013) Fiscal fan charts – a tool for assessing member states' (Likely?) Compliance with EU fiscal rules. *Fiscal Studies* 34(4): 517–34.

Darvas, Z. (2014) Does money matter in the Euro area? Evidence from a new Divisia index. Bruegel Working Paper.

Dittmar, R., Gavin, W. T. and Kydland, F. E. (1999) *Price-Level Uncertainty and Inflation Targeting. Federal Reserve Bank of St Louis Review* 81(4): 23–33.

Dittmar, R. and Gavin, W. T. (2000) What do New-Keynesian Phillips curves imply for price-level targeting? *Federal Reserve Bank of St Louis Review* 82(2): 21–30.

Dowd, K. (1995) Deflating the productivity norm. *Journal of Macroeconomics* 17(4): 717–32.

Dowd, K. (2004) The inflation 'fan charts': an evaluation. *Greek Economic Review* 23: 99–111.

Dowd, K. (2007a) Too good to be true? The (in)credibility of the UK inflation fan charts. *Journal of Macroeconomics* 29(1): 91–102.

Dowd, K. (2007b) Backtesting the RPIX inflation fan charts. *Journal of Risk Model Validation* 1(3): 1–19.

Dowd, K. (2008) The Swedish inflation fan charts: an evaluation of the Riksbank's inflation density forecasts. *Journal of Risk Model Validation* 2(1): 73–87.

Drew, S. and Dunn, M. (2011) Blue Book 2011: reclassification of the UK Supply and Use Tables. Office for National Statistics, November.

The Economist (2012a) Over the cliff? 15 December.

The Economist (2013a) The financial-repression levy, 23 March.

The Economist (2013b) Holding on for tomorrow, 16 November.

The Economist (2013c) Renouncing stable prices, 9 November.

The Economist (2013d) Where will the boot land next? 9 November.

The Economist (2014a) The once and future currency, 8 March.

Egger, J. B. (1994) The contributions of W. H. Hutt. *Review of Austrian Economics* 7(1): 107–38.

Egger, J. B. (1995) Arthur Marget in the Austrian tradition of the theory of money. *Review of Austrian Economics* 8(2): 3–23.

Estey, J. A. (1950) *Business Cycles: Their Nature, Cause, and Control.* New York: Prentice Hall.

Evans, A. J. (2013) Can we measure uncertainty? Kaleidic Economics Quarterly Report no. 7, March.

Evans, A. J. (2014) Welcome to the Great Stagnation. Kaleidic Economics Quarterly Report no. 11, March.

Evans, A. J. (2015) The financial crisis in the United Kingdom: uncertainty, calculation and error. In *The Oxford Handbook of Austrian Economics* (ed. C. J. Coyne and P. J. Boettke). Oxford University Press.

Evans, A. J. (2016a) *Sound Money: An Austrian Proposal for Free Banking, NGDP Targets, and OMO Reforms.* London: Adam Smith Institute.

Evans, A. J. (2016b) A dynamic AD-AS analysis of the UK economy 2002–2010. *Journal of Private Enterprise* 31(4): 97–105.

Evans, A. J. and Baxendale, T. (2010) The monetary contraction of 2008/09: assessing UK money supply measures in light of the financial crisis. Working paper, https://papers.ssrn.com/sol3/papers.cfm?abstract_id=1416922.

Evans, A. J. and Thorpe, R. (2013) The (quantity) theory of money and credit. *Review of Austrian Economics* 26(4): 463–81.

Ferguson, N. (2006) Friedman is dead, monetarism is dead, but what about inflation? *The Daily Telegraph*, 19 November 2006, http://www.telegraph.co.uk/opinion/main.jhtml?xml=/opinion/2006/11/19/do1904.xml (accessed 27 March 2015).

Findlay, S. (2001) *Prescription Drugs and Mass Media Advertising, 2000*. Washington, DC: National Institute for Health Care Management, Research and Educational Foundation.

Fisher, I. (1911) *The Purchasing Power of Money: Its Determination and Relation to Credit, Interest and Crises*. New York: Macmillan.

Fisher, I. (1933) The debt-deflation theory of great depressions. *Econometrica* 1(4): 337–357.

Fleming, M. H., Roman, J. and Farrell, G. (2000) The shadow economy. *Journal of International Affairs* 53(2): 387–409.

Friedman, M. (1956) *Studies in the Quantity Theory of Money*. University of Chicago Press.

Friedman, M. (1963) *Inflation: Causes and Consequences*. Bombay: Asia Publishing House for the Council for Economic Education.

Friedman, M. (1987) The quantity theory of money. In *The New Palgrave – Money*. London: Macmillan.

Friedman, M. and Schwartz, A. J. (1963a) Money and business cycles. In *The Optimum Quantity of Money and Other Essays*. Chicago University Press.

Friedman, M., and Schwartz, A. J. (1963b) *A Monetary History of the United States, 1867–1960*. Princeton University Press.

Friedman, M. and Schwartz, A. J. (1970) *Monetary Statistics of the United States: Estimates, Sources, Methods*. New York: Columbia University Press.

Garrison, R. (2001) *Time and Money. The Macroeconomics of Capital Structure*. New York: Routledge.

Geloso, V. (2015) Don't target NGDP, target NGO. Notes on Liberty, https://notesonliberty.com/2015/12/28/dont-target-ngdp -target-ngo/ (accessed 29 August 2016).

Geloso, V. (2016) NGO v. NGDP: in reply to Nunes and Sumner. Notes on Liberty, https://notesonliberty.com/2016/01/14/ngo-v-ngdp-in-reply-to-nunes-and-sumner/ (accessed 29 August 2016).

Giles, C. (2011) 'Formula effect' plays havoc with inflation figures. *Financial Times*, 15 November.

Goodhart, C. (2001) What weight should be given to asset prices in the measurement of inflation? *Economic Journal* 111(472): F335–F356.

Goodhart, C. (2007) Whatever became of the monetary aggregates. LSE Financial Markets Group Paper Series, http://www.lse.ac.uk/fmg/documents/specialPapers/2007/sp172.pdf (accessed 27 August 2016).

Greenspan, A. (2011) Activism. *International Finance* 14(1): 165–82.

Greenwood, J. (2006) Monetary policy and the Bank of Japan. In *Issues in Monetary Policy* (ed. P. Booth and K. Matthews). John Wiley & Sons.

Groth, C., Gutierrez-Domenach, M. and Srinvasan, S. (2004) Measuring total factor productivity for the United Kingdom. *Bank of England Quarterly Bulletin.*

Haberler (1996) Money and the business cycle. In *The Austrian Theory of the Trade Cycle and Other Essays* (ed. R. M. Ebeling). Auburn, AL: Mises Institute.

Hadley, J., Holahan, J. and Sanlon, W. (1979) Can fee-for-service reimbursement coexist with demand creation? *Enquiry* 16(3): 247–58.

Hamberg, D. (1951) *Business Cycles.* New York: Macmillan.

Hamilton, J. (2006) M2 and inflation. Econbrowser, 28 May.

Hamilton, J. (2008) Shadowstats responds. Econbrowser, 12 October, http://econbrowser.com/archives/2008/10/shadowstats_res (accessed 27 March 2015).

Hancock, M. (2005) Divisia money. *Bank of England Quarterly Bulletin*, 7 April.

Hanke, S. (2014) GO: J. M. Keynes versus J.-B. Say. *GlobeAsia*, July: 16–18.

Hayek, F. A. (2008) [1931/1935] *Prices and Production*. Auburn, AL: Ludwig von Mises Institute.

Heath, A. (2014) Everything we thought we knew about the economy was wrong. *Daily Telegraph*, 3 September.

Hendrickson, J. R. (2013) Redundancy or mismeasurement? a reappraisal of money. *Macroeconomic Dynamics* 18(7): 1437–65.

Higgs, R. (1997) Regime uncertainty: why the Great Depression lasted so long and why prosperity resumed after the war. *Independent Review* 1(4): 561–90.

Higgs, R. (2011) Regime uncertainty: Pirrong debunks the Keynesian debunking. The Beacon Blog, 5 September.

Hobijn, B. and Steindel, C. (2009) Do alternative measures of GDP affect its interpretation? Current Issues in Economics and Finance, Federal Reserve Bank of New York, 15(7).

Horwitz, S. (1990) A subjectivist approach to the demand for money. *Journal des Economistes et des Etudes Humaines* 1(4): 459–71.

Horwitz, S. (1994) Complementary non-quantity theory approaches to money: Hilferding's finance capital and free-banking theory. *History of Political Economy* 26(2): 221–38.

Horwitz, S. (2000) *Microfoundations and Macroeconomics: An Austrian Perspective*. New York: Routledge.

Horwitz, S. (2006) Monetary disequilibrium theory and Austrian macroeconomics: further thoughts on a synthesis. In *Money and Markets: Essays in Honour of Leland Yeager* (ed. R. Koppl). New York: Routledge.

Howden, D. (2013) The quantity theory of money. *Journal of Prices and Markets* 1(1): 17–30.

Hummel, J. R. (2011) Ben Bernanke versus Milton Friedman. *Independent Review* 15(4): 485–518.

Hummel, J. R. (2014) Fractional reserve banking and Austrian business cycle theory, http://oll.libertyfund.org/pages/misest mc#conversation4 (accessed 24 August 2016).

Hutt, W. H. (1956) The yield from money held. In *On Freedom and Free Enterprise: Essays in Honor of Ludwig von Mises* (ed. M. Sennholz). Princeton: Van Nostrand.

Hutt, W. H. (1963) *The Theory of Collective Bargaining*. London: P. S. King and Sons.

IMF (1993) *System of National Accounts*. Washington, DC.

IMF (2008) *Monetary and Financial Statistics: Compilation Guide*. Washington, DC.

Janssen, N. (2009) Measures of M4 and M4 lending excluding intermediate other financial corporations. Bank of England Monetary and Financial Statistics, May 2009.

Kaleidic Economics (2012) Important updates to MA compilation, 23 January, http://www.kaleidic.org/news/2012/1/23/im portant-updates-to-ma-compilation.html (accessed 25 May 2014).

Kaleidic Economics (2014) First glance at MAex. 2 July, http://www.kaleidic.org/news/2014/7/2/first-glance-at-m4ex.html (accessed 24 August 2016).

Keynes, J. M. (1923) *A Tract on Monetary Reform*. London: Macmillan.

Keynes, J. M. (1963) [1925] The economic consequences of Mr Churchill. In *Essays in Persuasion*. New York: W. W. Norton.

Knight, F. (1921) *Risk, Uncertainty and Profit*. Boston: Houghton Mifflin.

Koppl, R. (2002) *Big Players and the Economic Theory of Expectations*. Basingstoke: Palgrave Macmillan.

Koppl, R. and Yeager, L. (1996) Big players and herding in asset markets: the case of the Russian ruble. *Explorations in Russian History* 33(3): 367–83.

Kryvtsov, O., Shukayev, M. and Ueberfeldt, A. (2008) Adopting price-level targeting under imperfect credibility: an update. Bank of Canada Working Paper 2008-37.

Kuznets, S. (1934) National Income, 1929–32. Bulletin 49. New York: National Bureau of Economic Research.

Labelle, R., Stoddart, G. and Rise, T. (1994) A re-examination of the meaning and importance of supplier-induced demand. *Journal of Health Economics* 13(3): 347–68.

Lachmann, L. (1978) An Austrian stocktaking: unsettled question and tentative answers. In *New Directions in Austrian Economics* (ed. L. M. Sporado). Kansas City: Sheed, Andrews and McMeel.

Laidler, D. (1977) [1969] *The Demand for Money: Theories and Evidence*. New York: Dun-Donnelley.

Laidler, D. (1989) Radcliffe, the quantity theory and monetarism. In *Money, Trade and Payments: Essays in Honour of Dennis Coppock* (ed. D. R. Cobham, R. Harrington and G. Zis). University of Manchester Press.

Laidler, D. (1991) The quantity theory is always and everywhere controversial – why? *Economic Record* 67(4): 289–306.

Landefield, J. S., Seskin, E. P. and Fraumeni, B. M. (2008) Taking the pulse of the economy: measuring GDP. *Journal of Economic Perspectives* 22(2): 193–216.

Leduc, S. and Zheng, L. (2012) Uncertainty, unemployment, and inflation. FRBSF Economic Letter, 17 September.

Leduc, S. and Zheng, L. (2013) Uncertainty and the slow labor market recovery. FRBSF Economic Letter, 22 July.

Lilico, A. (2009a) *What Killed Capitalism? The Crisis: What Caused It and How to Respond.* London: Centre for Policy Studies.

Lilico, A. (2009b) On the merits of price-level targeting. In *Beyond Inflation Targeting: The New Paradigm for Central Bank Policy* (ed. H. Thomas). London: Policy Exchange.

Littlechild, S. (2000) Disreputable adventures: the Shackle papers at Cambridge. In *Economics as an Art of Thought: Essays in Memory of G. L. S. Shackle* (ed. P. E. Earl and S. F. Frowen). London: Routledge.

Lucas, R. E. (1972) Expectations and the neutrality of money. *Journal of Economic Theory* 4(2): 103–24.

Lucas, R. E. (1975) An equilibrium model of the business cycle. *Journal of Political Economy* 83(61): 1113–44.

Luther, W. (2016) Mises and the moderns on the inessentiality of money in equilibrium. *Review of Austrian Economics* 29(1): 1–13.

Machlup, F. (1935) Professor Knight and the 'period of production'. *Journal of Political Economy* 43(5): 577–624.

Mankiw, N. G. (2002) *Macroeconomics*, 2nd edn. New York: Worth.

Marget, A. W. (1937) Inflation, inevitable or avoidable? Lecture presented on 23 November 1936 at the University of Minnesota. Published as no. 15 in the University's 'Day and Hour Series'. University of Minnesota Press, January 1937.

Marget, A. W. (1942) *The Theory of Prices: A Re-Examination of the Central Problems of Monetary Theory*, Vol. 2. New York: Prentice-Hall.

McCulloch, J. H. (1975) *Money and Inflation: A Monetarist Approach*. New York: Academic Press.

McLeay, M., Radia, A. and Thomas, R. (2014) Money creation in the modern economy. *Bank of England Quarterly Bulletin* Q1: 14–27.

Meltzer, A. H. (2012) Federal Reserve policy in the Great Recession. *Cato Journal* 32(2): 255–63.

Menger, C. (1892) On the origins of money. *Economic Journal* 2(6): 239–55.

Mills, F. C. (1946) *Price-Quantity Interactions in Business Cycles*. New York: NBER.

Mises, L. v. (1980) [1912] *The Theory of Money and Credit*. Indianapolis: Liberty Fund.

Mises, L. v. (1996) [1949] *Human Action: A Treatise on Economics*. New York: Foundation for Economic Education.

Munro, J. (2007) Review Essay of Hamilton, E. J. (1934) *American Treasure and the Price Revolution in Spain, 1501–1650*. Cambridge, MA: Harvard University Press. EH.net, http://eh.net/book_reviews/american-treasure-and-the-price-revolution-in-spain-1501–1650/ (accessed 31 July 2014).

Nunes, M. and Cole, B. M. (2013) *Market Monetarism: Roadmap to Economic Prosperity*. CreateSpace Independent Publishing Platform.

O'Driscoll, G. P. and Rizzo, M. J. (1996) [1985] *The Economics of Time and Ignorance*. New York: Routledge.

O'Mahony, M. and Timmer, M. P. (2009) Output, input and productivity measures at the industry level: the EU KLEMS database. *Economic Journal* 119(538): F374–F403.

Oulton, N. and Srinivasan, S. (2003) Capital stocks, capital services, and depreciation: an integrated framework. Bank of England Working Paper no. 192.

Patinkin, D. (1965) *Money, Interest, and Prices*, 2nd edn. New York: Harper and Row.

Paulson, H. (2010) *On the Brink. Inside the Race to Stop the Collapse of the Global Financial System*. New York: Business Plus.

Peston, R. (2008) *Who Runs Britain?* London: Hodder & Stoughton.

Phillips, C. A., McManus, T. F. and Nelson, R. W. (2007) [1937] *Banking and the Business Cycle – A Study of the Great Depression in the United States*. New York: Macmillan.

Pollaro, M. (2010) Money supply metrics, the Austrian take. Mises Daily, https://mises.org/library/money-supply-metrics -austrian-take (accessed 24 August 2016).

Posen, A. (2011) Monetary policy, bubbles, and the knowledge problem. *Cato Journal* 31(3): 461–73.

Prasad, E. (2014) *The Dollar Trap. How the U.S. Dollar Tightened Its Grip on Global Finance*. Princeton University Press.

Radford, R. A. (1945) The economic organization of a P.O.W. camp. *Economica* 12(48): 189–201.

Ranson, R. D. (2015) Alternative data to track the economy and better explain capital-market prices. HCWE Worldwide Economics Economy Watch, 3 November.

Reisman, G. (1990) *Capitalism: A Treatise on Economics*. Ottawa, IL: Jameson Books

Restieaux, A. (2013) *Introducing the New CPIH Measure of Consumer Price Inflation*. London: Office for National Statistics.

Romer, C. D. (1992) What ended the Great Depression? *Journal of Economic History* 52(4): 757–84.

Rothbard, M. N. (1963) *America's Great Depression*. Kansas City: Sheed and Ward.

Rothbard, M. N. (1978) Austrian definitions of the supply of money. In *New Directions in Austrian Economics* (ed. L. M. Spadaro). Kansas City: Sheed Andrews and McMeel.

Salerno, J. T. (1987) The 'true' money supply: a measure of the supply of the medium of exchange in the U.S. economy. Austrian Economics Newsletter, Ludwig von Mises Institute.

Salter, A. W. (2013) Not all NGDP is created equal: a critique of market monetarism. *Journal of Private Enterprise* 24(1): 41–53.

Samuelson, P. and Nordhaus, W. (2009) [1948] *Economics*. Columbus, OH: McGraw-Hill Education.

Sanderson, R., Clews, G. and Winterton, J. (2014) Calculating a Laspeyres version of the UK consumer prices index. Office for National Statistics.

Schneider, F. and Enste, D. H. (2002) *The Shadow Economy: An International Survey*. Cambridge University Press.

Selgin, G. (1988) *The Theory of Free Banking*. Lanham, MD: Rowman & Littlefield.

Selgin, G. (1995) The case for a 'productivity norm': comment on Dowd. *Journal of Macroeconomics* 17(4): 733–40.

Selgin, G. (1997) *Less than Zero: The Case for a Falling Price Level in a Growing Economy*. London: Institute of Economic Affairs.

Selgin, G. (2012) How? Alt-M, 17 September, https://www.alt-m.org/2012/09/17/how/ (accessed 6 April 2018).

Sentance, A. (2012) Weak GDP figures won't mean the economy is about to fall off a cliff. *City AM*, 23 July.

Simons, H. C. (1938) *Personal Income Taxation: The Definition of Income as a Problem of Fiscal Policy.* University of Chicago Press.

Shelton, J. (2012) Gold and government. *Cato Journal* 32(2): 333–49.

Shostak, F. (1999) Asian recovery? *Asian Wall Street Journal*, 15 June.

Shostak, F. (2000) The mystery of the money supply definition. *Quarterly Journal of Austrian Economics* 3(4): 69–76.

Skousen, M. (2007) [1990] *The Structure of Production.* New York University Press.

Skousen, M. (2010) Gross domestic expenditures (GDE): the need for a new aggregate statistic. Working Paper.

Skousen, M. (2013) Has government adopted my new macro model? MSkousen.com, 4 October.

Skousen, M. (2014) At last, a better economic measure. *Wall Street Journal*, 23 April.

Skousen, M. (2016) GO beyond GSP: introducing gross output as a top-line in national income accounting. Working Paper.

Smith, A. (1904) [1776] *An Inquiry into the Nature and Causes of the Wealth of Nations*, 5th edn. London: Methuen.

Smith, D. B. (2010) Money still matters: the implications of M4X for quantitative easing. IEA Discussion Paper 26. London: Institute of Economic Affairs.

Solow, R. M. (1957) Technical change and the aggregate production function. *Review of Economics and Statistics* 39(3): 312–20.

Stein, L. and Stone, E. (2012) The effect of uncertainty on investment, hiring, and R&D: causal evidence from equity options. Working paper, Arizona State University.

Sumner, S. (2016) NGDP or NGO? Money illusion, http://econlog .econlib.org/archives/2016/01/ngdp_or_ngo.html   (accessed 23 August 2016).

Svensson, L. E. O. (1999) Price level targeting vs. inflation targeting: a free lunch? *Journal of Money, Credit and Banking* 31(3): 277–95.

Teles, P. and Zhou, R. (2005) A stable money demand: looking for the right monetary aggregate. Federal Reserve Bank of Chicago. *Economic Perspectives* Q1: 50–93.

Thomas, H. (ed.) (2009) *Beyond Inflation Targeting: The New Paradigm for Central Bank Policy.* London: Policy Exchange.

Turvey A. (2009) Multi-factor productivity: estimates for 1998 to 2007. *Economics and Labour Market Review* 3(3): 33–38.

U.S. Department of Commerce (1975) *Historical Statistics of the United States.* Washington, DC.

van Overtveldt, J. (2007) *The Chicago School. How the University of Chicago Assembled the Thinkers Who Revolutionized Economics and Business.* Evanston, IL: Agate Publishing.

Wallis, K. F. (2003) Chi-squared tests of interval and density forecasts, and the Bank of England's fan charts. *International Journal of Forecasting* 19(2): 165–75.

Wallis, K. F. (2004) An assessment of Bank of England and National Institute inflation forecast uncertainties. *National Institute Economic Review* 189(1): 64–71.

Wallison, P. J. (2011) Three narratives about the financial crisis. *Cato Journal* 31(3): 535–49.

Walters, B. (2008) *The Fall of Northern Rock: An Insider's Story of Britain's Biggest Banking Disaster.* Petersfield: Harriman House.

Ward, S. (2011) Pull the other one, Gov. Money Moves Markets, 7 October.

Wen, Y. and Arias, M. A. (2014) What does money velocity tell us about low inflation in the US? Federal Reserve Bank of St Louis, On the Economy Blog, 1 September.

White, L. H. (1992) *Competition and Currency: Essays on Free Banking and Money.* New York University Press.

White, L. H. (1999) *The Theory of Monetary Institutions.* Oxford: Blackwell.

White, L. H. (2005) The Federal Reserve System's influence on research in monetary economics. *Econ Journal Watch* 2(2): 325–54.

White, L. H. (2010) The rule of law or the rule of central bankers? *Cato Journal* 30(3): 451–63.

White, W. R. (2010) Comments on 'After the Fall' by C. and V. Reinhart. Symposium on 'Macroeconomic Challenges: The Decade Ahead'. Federal Reserve Bank of Kansas City, Jackson Hole Wyoming.

White, W. R. (2012) Ultra easy monetary policy and the law of unintended consequences. Federal Reserve Bank of Dallas, Working Paper 126.

Woods, T. E. (2008) What Austrian economics can teach historians. *Quarterly Journal of Austrian Economics* 11(3): 219–29.

Yeager, L. B. (1997) *The Fluttering Veil: Essays on Monetary Disequilibrium.* Liberty Fund.

ABOUT THE IEA

The Institute is a research and educational charity (No. CC 235 351), limited by guarantee. Its mission is to improve understanding of the fundamental institutions of a free society by analysing and expounding the role of markets in solving economic and social problems.

The IEA achieves its mission by:

- a high-quality publishing programme
- conferences, seminars, lectures and other events
- outreach to school and college students
- brokering media introductions and appearances

The IEA, which was established in 1955 by the late Sir Antony Fisher, is an educational charity, not a political organisation. It is independent of any political party or group and does not carry on activities intended to affect support for any political party or candidate in any election or referendum, or at any other time. It is financed by sales of publications, conference fees and voluntary donations.

In addition to its main series of publications, the IEA also publishes (jointly with the University of Buckingham), *Economic Affairs*.

The IEA is aided in its work by a distinguished international Academic Advisory Council and an eminent panel of Honorary Fellows. Together with other academics, they review prospective IEA publications, their comments being passed on anonymously to authors. All IEA papers are therefore subject to the same rigorous independent refereeing process as used by leading academic journals.

IEA publications enjoy widespread classroom use and course adoptions in schools and universities. They are also sold throughout the world and often translated/reprinted.

Since 1974 the IEA has helped to create a worldwide network of 100 similar institutions in over 70 countries. They are all independent but share the IEA's mission.

Views expressed in the IEA's publications are those of the authors, not those of the Institute (which has no corporate view), its Managing Trustees, Academic Advisory Council members or senior staff.

Members of the Institute's Academic Advisory Council, Honorary Fellows, Trustees and Staff are listed on the following page.

The Institute gratefully acknowledges financial support for its publications programme and other work from a generous benefaction by the late Professor Ronald Coase.

Other books recently published by the IEA include:

Flaws and Ceilings – Price Controls and the Damage They Cause
Edited by Christopher Coyne and Rachel Coyne
Hobart Paperback 179; ISBN 978-0-255-36701-1; £12.50

Scandinavian Unexceptionalism: Culture, Markets and the Failure of Third-Way Socialism
Nima Sanandaji
Readings in Political Economy 1; ISBN 978-0-255-36704-2; £10.00

Classical Liberalism – A Primer
Eamonn Butler
Readings in Political Economy 2; ISBN 978-0-255-36707-3; £10.00

Federal Britain: The Case for Decentralisation
Philip Booth
Readings in Political Economy 3; ISBN 978-0-255-36713-4; £10.00

Forever Contemporary: The Economics of Ronald Coase
Edited by Cento Veljanovski
Readings in Political Economy 4; ISBN 978-0-255-36710-3; £15.00

Power Cut? How the EU Is Pulling the Plug on Electricity Markets
Carlo Stagnaro
Hobart Paperback 180; ISBN 978-0-255-36716-5; £10.00

Policy Stability and Economic Growth – Lessons from the Great Recession
John B. Taylor
Readings in Political Economy 5; ISBN 978-0-255-36719-6; £7.50

Breaking Up Is Hard To Do: Britain and Europe's Dysfunctional Relationship
Edited by Patrick Minford and J. R. Shackleton
Hobart Paperback 181; ISBN 978-0-255-36722-6; £15.00

In Focus: The Case for Privatising the BBC
Edited by Philip Booth
Hobart Paperback 182; ISBN 978-0-255-36725-7; £12.50

Islamic Foundations of a Free Society
Edited by Nouh El Harmouzi and Linda Whetstone
Hobart Paperback 183; ISBN 978-0-255-36728-8; £12.50

The Economics of International Development: Foreign Aid versus Freedom for the World's Poor
William Easterly
Readings in Political Economy 6; ISBN 978-0-255-36731-8; £7.50

Other IEA publications

Comprehensive information on other publications and the wider work of the IEA can be found at www.iea.org.uk. To order any publication please see below.

Personal customers

Orders from personal customers should be directed to the IEA:

Clare Rusbridge
IEA
2 Lord North Street
FREEPOST LON10168
London SW1P 3YZ
Tel: 020 7799 8907. Fax: 020 7799 2137
Email: sales@iea.org.uk

Trade customers

All orders from the book trade should be directed to the IEA's distributor:

NBN International (IEA Orders)
Orders Dept.
NBN International
10 Thornbury Road
Plymouth PL6 7PP
Tel: 01752 202301, Fax: 01752 202333
Email: orders@nbninternational.com

IEA subscriptions

The IEA also offers a subscription service to its publications. For a single annual payment (currently £42.00 in the UK), subscribers receive every monograph the IEA publishes. For more information please contact:

Clare Rusbridge
Subscriptions
IEA
2 Lord North Street
FREEPOST LON10168
London SW1P 3YZ
Tel: 020 7799 8907, Fax: 020 7799 2137
Email: crusbridge@iea.org.uk